Find Your Story,
Write Your Memoir

Find Your Story,
Write Your Memoir

Lynn C. Miller *and* Lisa Lenard-Cook

THE UNIVERSITY OF WISCONSIN PRESS

The University of Wisconsin Press
1930 Monroe Street, 3rd Floor
Madison, Wisconsin 53711-2059
uwpress.wisc.edu

3 Henrietta Street
London WC2E 8LU, England
eurospanbookstore.com

Printed in the United States of America

Library of Congress Cataloging-in-Publication Data

Miller, Lynn, 1951–
Find your story, write your memoir / Lynn C. Miller and Lisa Lenard-Cook.
p.   cm.
Includes bibliographical references.
ISBN 978-0-299-29314-7 (pbk. : alk. paper) — ISBN 978-0-299-29313-0 (e-book)
1. Autobiography—Authorship. I. Lenard-Cook, Lisa. II. Title.
CT25.M484   2013
808.06′692—dc23
2012032685

Excerpts from *The Memory Palace: A Memoir* by Mira Bartók, copyright © 2011 by Mira Bartók,
are reprinted by permission of Free Press, a division of Simon & Schuster Inc. Excerpts from
The Walk by William deBuys are reprinted by permission of Trinity University Press. Excerpts
from *The Year of Magical Thinking* by Joan Didion, copyright © 2005 by Joan Didion, are
reprinted by permission of Alfred A. Knopf, a division of Random House, Inc. Excerpts from
An American Childhood by Annie Dillard, copyright © 1987 by Annie Dillard, are reprinted by
permission of HarperCollins Publishers. Excerpts from *Heaven's Coast: A Memoir* by Mark Doty,
copyright © 1996 by Mark Doty, are reprinted by permission of HarperCollins Publishers.
Excerpts from *The Situation and the Story: The Art of Personal Narrative* by Vivian Gornick,
copyright © 2001 by Vivian Gornick, are reprinted by permission of Farrar, Straus and Giroux.
Excerpts from *The Liars' Club: A Memoir* by Mary Karr, copyright © 1995 by Mary Karr, are
reprinted by permission of Penguin Group. Excerpts from *Oleander, Jacaranda: A Childhood
Perceived* by Penelope Lively, copyright © 1994 by Penelope Lively, are reprinted by permission
of HarperCollins Publishers. Excerpts from *Searching for Mercy Street: My Journey Back to
My Mother, Anne Sexton* by Linda Gray Sexton, copyright © 1994 by Linda Gray Sexton, are
reprinted by permission of the author. Excerpts from *Fearless Confessions: A Writer's Guide
to Memoir* by Sue William Silverman, copyright © 2009 by Sue William Silverman, are
reprinted by permission of the University of Georgia Press. Excerpts from *This Boy's Life*,
copyright © 1989 by Tobias Wolf, are reprinted by permission of Grove/Atlantic, Inc.

Contents

Preface

What are the ingredients for a memoir that resonates with readers? It's not just story—although when someone like Jeanette Walls or Mira Bartók triumphs in the face of a challenging childhood and adolescence, the reader can't help but cheer.

It's not just voice—although when someone like Tobias Wolff or Mary Karr shares his or her family stories, the reader can't help but empathize.

Nor is it merely the universality of any author's particular story—although when Joan Didion examines her first year as a widow, the reader is riveted and grieves along with her.

What keeps us turning the pages of *Eat, Pray, Love*; *Just Kids*; *Angela's Ashes*; and scores of other breakout memoirs is the way each author uses powerful storytelling strategies—what we call the "Fiction Writer's Toolkit" for memoir—to find her or his story.

We come to this book after years of teaching memoir and even more years as fiction writers. While Lisa has written dozens of books of nonfiction and Lynn has worked in autobiographical performance for two decades, our philosophy in *Find Your Story, Write Your Memoir* is that key word: *story*.

Our work with students has shown us that while every person has a story to tell, few know, when they first set out, how to uncover its narrative potential or how to unleash its power.

That's the catalyst behind the Fiction Writer's Toolkit, the method that illuminates our theory and practice. In these pages, we'll illustrate the difference between life events and a dynamic structure and plot that keep the reader glued to the pages or the screen. In this book, we'll guide you, the author, through the beginning impulse to write your story, what we call *the occasion of the telling*, on to the dance of memory and experience, through plot, structure, character, landscape, and scene. Along the way, spotlight writing and reading exercises will help you to develop sections of your memoir as you explore the theory and practice we've developed through extensive analysis of both classic and contemporary memoirs and fiction.

We invite you to find your story as we take you through the process.

CHAPTER 1. THE OCCASION OF THE TELLING: "IT BEGINS HERE BECAUSE IT'S ABOUT THIS"

A memoir's opening pages set up the urgency and risk of telling this particular story at this particular moment. Whether there's a deathbed confession or a Proustian madeleine, something in the "present" compels the author to revisit the past. In this chapter, we show the writer how she can best answer the question, "Why this story now?"

CHAPTER 2. THE TWO YOUS: FINDING A PLACE TO STAND

The memoir is told by an author in the present (the remembering self) who takes the reader to various stages of her past (the experiencing self). The journey of this past self—along with its lessons and conflicts—gives the story its tension and informs the author in the present. Because of the dual nature of memoir, the story is a journey of self-discovery not only for the author but for the reader as well. We'll also explore the challenges and pleasures of this duality.

CHAPTER 3. BUILDING A NARRATIVE: LAYING DOWN THE BONES

There are as many ways of constructing a memoir as there are individual stories. This chapter explores the many possible ways of arranging a story, the ways plot and structure intertwine, and provides tools for finding the structure appropriate to the author's particular narrative. Structures explored include chronological, circular, associative, collage, parallel, and locational. In addition, readers will learn the importance of beginning a story with catalyst and conflict and how to map the tension.

CHAPTER 4. ARRANGING THE SCENES: GIVING THEM MUSCLE

Yes, it really happened, but in order to re-create a scene for readers, authors must be aware of dramatic urgency. That's why this chapter focuses on scene building. We look at traditional dramatic scenes, how internal scenes can rise in action via conflict and drama, the importance of silence and gaps for the reader to fill, and the use of dialogue as action.

CHAPTER 5. PAINTING THE PICTURE: LANGUAGE AND SETTING

Plots for memoirs focus not only on the character telling the story but also on the actions of secondary characters, the use of landscape and setting—and the seemingly random moments in a life. The telling detail, the dominant image, sustaining metaphors and leitmotifs, and a sense of place provide a layering of the story scaffolding that adds texture and complexity to the memoir.

CHAPTER 6. YOUR STORY, YOUR VOICE: MAKE IT YOUR OWN

Every writer has his own unique style and voice. In the case of the memoir, style and voice inform the story being told as the author views his remembered self with compassion, humor, and even forgiveness. This chapter explores the voices and styles in breakout memoirs and gives writers tools to develop authentic voices of their own.

CHAPTER 7. HONORING THE MEMOIR PROCESS: TAKING THE NEXT STEPS

You've written a chapter or more of your memoir, or perhaps you've finished the essay or book you wanted to write. As you look at what you've produced, you already feel a distance between the impulse that motivated you to begin writing and your self in the present. No matter how often we rewrite or how polished our product is, we question whether it's of interest to others and whether we've captured our authentic journey. This chapter discusses the ethics of telling your own story, suggests possibilities for revision strategies and ways of getting your work out in front of readers, and sums up the value of the memoir-writing process.

We've tested our ideas in classes, workshops, and retreats as well as in our own writing, and we have found that our approach provides the lightbulb moments memoir writers are seeking. We're thrilled to be sharing the Fiction Writer's Toolkit with you, and we hope it will help you take your memoir to the next level.

Acknowledgments

We'd like to express our appreciation to our acquisitions editor, Raphael Kadushin, who stood behind this book all the way. In addition, the rest of the team at the University of Wisconsin Press, in particular Matthew Cosby, made the process a pleasure at every step.

Thanks also go to the students in our writing courses taught in Albuquerque from 2010 through 2012, especially Jill Root, Carol March, and Alice Brasfield. Your courage and probing questions inspired this book.

As always, we're grateful to our spouses Lynda and Bob for their support.

Find Your Story,
Write Your Memoir

1

The Occasion of the Telling

"It Begins Here because It's about This"

Memoir begins not with event but with the intuition of meaning—with the mysterious fact that life can sometimes step free from the chaos of contingency and become story.

—SVEN BIRKERTS, *The Art of Time in Memoir: Then, Again*

Find Your Story, Write Your Memoir focuses on enhancing your narrative by using the Fiction Writer's Toolkit. In these pages, we'll show you how the elements of craft will take your story from the jumble that is memory and circumstance into a story that has expressive characters, evocative descriptions, an organic structure, and a singular voice. By the time you finish, you'll possess all the tools required to turn events that happened to you into a skillfully told story.

The fact that you want to write a memoir at all indicates that you're interested in the journey of self-discovery, a key to the telling of all stories, whether fiction or nonfiction. A memoir details a specific journey in your life rather than the arc of your entire life. However, even though the memoir highlights a particular series of events, it forces you the writer to view your past through the lens of the telling of this significant life event as well. Our question for this chapter is: What stimulates the desire to write a memoir? Determining the spark or trigger that releases your story is your first task in beginning to write.

Here's the beginning of Joan Didion's haunting memoir *The Year of Magical Thinking*:

Life changes fast.
Life changes in the instant.
You sit down to dinner and life as you know it ends.
The question of self pity.

Those were the first words I wrote after it happened. . . . For a long time I wrote nothing else. (3)

Why does this story begin here? Or, to put it another way, what in the author's *now* has compelled her to revisit this particular *then*? This is what we mean when we refer to *the occasion of the telling*.

The occasion of the telling answers the question,
Why is *this* story being told now?

A memoir's opening pages set up *the urgency or risk of telling this particular story at this particular moment.* Whether there's a deathbed confession or a Proustian madeleine, something in an author's "present" compels him or her to revisit the past. In this chapter, we show how you can best answer the question "Why this story now?" for your own story.

A PLACE TO STAND

It's not enough that something happened, something life-changing, something devastating, something, in Didion's case, like the death of a loved one. What distinguishes the best memoirs is who we are in time and space when we *revisit* those life-changing events. This "now" of the narrator isn't about a date on the calendar, or even the author's present, but rather a state of mind and emotion, *a place to stand* from which you write about an event that has shaped your life to this point.

Hence, Joan Didion begins *The Year of Magical Thinking* where she does because it's at this moment that she opens the notes she made a few days after her husband, novelist John Gregory Dunne, died in January 2004 in order to begin to explore what happened at that moment and—more important for her story—what happened afterward. Didion couldn't have written this memoir while it was happening because she needed narrative distance from the time John died before she could begin to try to write about it. When you try to write about something while you're still living through it, you lack perspective—and writing a memoir is all about having perspective.

Thus, like Didion, your first step in determining your story's occasion of the telling is to understand that writing a memoir requires what we like to call the *two yous*: who you are *now*, looking back at what happened with whatever insight compelled you to begin writing (the occasion of the telling);

and who you were *then*—younger, perhaps not so wise, but living through those moments.

Another way of looking at the two yous is to think of one as the self who's *remembering*—the narrator who provides the continuity throughout the book—and the other as the self who's *experiencing* scenes in the past at distinct times. The interaction between these two yous is what propels your story forward. We'll look at this concept in depth in chapter 2.

The *two yous* refers to you, the remembering self, now,
and you, the experiencing self, then.

Here are two more ways to understand the occasion of the telling and the two yous. After we explained these two concepts to one of our classes, a clever student piped up, "It begins here because it's about this." Another added, "I need to have a place to stand to tell this story." The place to stand represents the remembering narrator. Where the remembering narrator stands is not necessarily when in actual time the author is writing but rather a place she has chosen because it's cathartic. The catharsis itself leads the author to the occasion of the telling.

Catharsis refers to the release of emotion (often long-buried). Aristotle writes in his *Poetics* how cathartic events in a play allow the audience to expel repressed or intense feeling. Similarly, readers are attracted to stories that allow them to explore their own life challenges, that help them grasp the significance in archetypal tales of crisis and redemption. The hero's journey (the mythic path to self-discovery) itself always begins with an occasion of the telling. Something occurs that thrusts the protagonist into a new space. For example, the goddess Demeter, who controls the earth's bounty, created the seasons when she lost her daughter, Persephone. For the months Persephone must spend in Hades, Demeter mourns, and winter falls upon the earth. When her daughter returns, Demeter's joy is represented by spring.

In the memoir you are about to write, you are the hero, and the journey is yours. We suggest that you refer to Joseph Campbell's wonderful books, which illuminate how the ancient myths are also myths for our time. As in mythologies from all cultures, most memoirs begin with loss or conflict, then detail the journey toward coming to terms with that loss or conflict. They represent the writer's attempt to understand key people in his or her life, often parents or spouses or siblings. For example, in Mira Bartók's *The Memory Palace*, the

protagonist receives a phone message about her mother, with whom the protagonist had ceased contact seventeen years before. The memory of the
missed phone call, a metaphor of broken connection, provides the catalyst for
the telling.

Similarly, Geoffrey Wolff's *The Duke of Deception: Memories of My Father*
opens with a premonition of death. Then the phone rings, and a relative
answers. Wolff, who's been imagining that the call will report the death of one
of his children, is audibly relieved to hear that it is his father who has died.
Wolff's ensuing guilt and shock over his own words punctuate the complexity
of his perceptions about this important figure in his life.

SPOTLIGHT EXERCISE

Writing: Think about stories that have resonated throughout your life. First,
choose an often-told family story: jot down a description of the central
character and how you came to hear about the story. Why do you think
this story was handed down in your family? What did it illustrate? Second,
note a story you've read, whether fiction or memoir, young adult or fable.
How does the story begin? What event or thought causes the hero to
make a break with the past or embark on a new path?

This exercise illustrates how the classic structure resonates in the stories
we've heard all our lives.

Considering stories you've always known from the perspective of why they
were told in the first place is a great first step toward discovering your own
story's occasion of the telling. For this reason, you may want to apply this
exercise to everything you read and hear for a while.

With the concepts of the occasion of the telling and the two yous in hand,
let's look more closely at what makes a memoir a memoir.

Is It an Autobiography, or Is It a Memoir?

As author/educator Sidonie Smith has noted, autobiography is a unique genre
because, in this form, the self becomes both subject and object. But, while
both memoir and autobiography are written by someone about him- or herself, the similarity between the two ends there.

Autobiographies are usually written toward the end of a public figure's life
and recount that life chronologically, beginning with the author's birth (or
sometimes with the author's parents' births). Fictive technique isn't as central

to autobiography, because readers read these books to find out about the author's entire life, often because the author is someone in whom the reader is interested in knowing more about: celebrity and fame create an audience all by themselves.

Autobiographies are also often told chronologically, which reduces the importance of decisions about structure, plot, and emphasis, all of which are important choices in memoir writing. In autobiography, issues like plot and scene are recorded as they occurred or are remembered rather than constructed by the writer to dramatize a particular journey. Simply put, an autobiography is a record of a life, while a memoir is an exploration of a specific aspect of a life, using fictive techniques to create a dynamic story.

An *autobiography* is a record of a life.

A *memoir* is an exploration of a significant time in a life using narrative strategies to create a dynamic story.

Memoirs *spotlight* (make a note of that word, because we'll be using it a lot in a number of different contexts) a period in the author's life distinguished in some unusual way. To broadly paraphrase Tolstoy, every family is dysfunctional, but each family's individual dysfunctionality contains the seeds of memoir. The memoirist revisits this crucial time (the revisiting, as noted above, is another distinguishing quality), applying acquired or newfound knowledge to those events in the past. The tension between the self who remembers and the past he or she revisits is a key to a memoir's plot, which we'll cover in depth in chapters 3 and 4.

It's about the Storyteller

We readers begin reading (any book—not just a memoir) because we're interested in the story. But when it comes to a memoir, we *keep* reading because we become invested in the storyteller. The risks he or she takes and their consequences immerse the reader in the memoirist's story—we keep reading because we find ourselves on a journey with a narrator about whom we come to care deeply.

Writing the memoir is in some ways like keeping one's balance atop a narrow fence: you need to present an honest appraisal of yourself, the main character in your memoir, while at the same time being the one who's telling the story. As with any character, the narrator makes mistakes and has flaws. It's how he or she negotiates these pitfalls that invest us in his or her story. Such an unflinching look at self and situation is what made Frank McCourt's *Angela's Ashes* (1996) and Jeannette Walls's *The Glass Castle* (2005) breakout memoirs.

Reliability and the Narrator

Because the writer is a character, we like to refer to the protagonist of the memoir the same way we do the narrator of fiction: as the *speaker* or *narrator*. We'd also like to encourage you to speak of the experiencing you you're writing about now in the same way. Doing so will offer you a narrative distance that will help you create a stronger narrative arc and more compelling characters—in the case of memoir, allowing you to dramatize specific people you know or have known. Thinking of yourself as a narrator creates a safe space around the events from which to create your story as well. The story is then allowed a life of its own. In this way, you create a distinction between you personally and the narrative you're creating.

> We use the term *speaker* or *narrator* when we discuss the voice that relates to a memoir in order to distance the writer from his or her characters, even or especially when the writer is a character.

Thinking of yourself and the others in your story as characters allows you to be less chained to the exact details of what happened and more open to the meaning and shape of what happened. After all, as we all know, memory not only is fallible but at each stage of our lives is reinterpreted, seen in a fresh and sometimes surprising light. The fact is, if you were to write about these same events in twenty years, it would likely be a very different story. To burrow deep into the *truth* of the story, we need to worry less about the chronological *exactness* of what happened and instead remain true to the story's larger truth.

At the same time, it's important that your memoir doesn't play with facts. You're likely familiar with the debates about whether memoirs are fact or fiction—for instance, the fracas around James Frey's *A Million Little Pieces* and whether events in Greg Mortensen's *Three Cups of Tea* actually happened. So, while readers of memoir understand that (for example) if dialogue appears, it's likely reconstructed, they won't tolerate the manufacturing of a reality that never occurred at all. Because the issue of truth in the memoir has been so hotly debated, we'll delve into it further here before we go on.

Telling the Truth in Memoir

In fiction and in memoir, one of the first decisions the reader makes is whether or not the storyteller is telling the truth. We call the storyteller we can trust a *reliable narrator*. In fiction, writers often use *unreliable narrators*, particularly in the first person, to show that a character's self-interest blinds him or her to a more measured view of a situation. For instance, in Eudora Welty's short story "Why I Live at the P.O.," the protagonist, outraged at the way she's been treated by her family, has moved to the post office, where she works, and is eager to tell her side of the story. Much of the humor in the story comes from her biased point of view and skewed sense of reality.

A *reliable narrator* appears to have a perspective in line with the values in the story and is someone the reader trusts to have a balanced view of the story.

An *unreliable narrator* deceives himself or the reader—his view of events does not mesh with the "facts" of what really happened. An unreliable narrator forces the reader to decide for herself what the story's truth really is.

Memory is notoriously unreliable, and our stories in memoir are *our* stories, no one else's. Many writers have weighed in on this issue, and the consensus is that, in memoir, the writer owes it to the reader to be as accurate as he or she can. However, given that we are each limited to what we experience and to the quality of our perceptions, here are several examples of reasoned opinions on the accuracy issue.

Judith Barrington, in *Writing the Memoir: From Truth to Art*, stresses how difficult it is to tell the truth and find the facts, along with the necessity of doing so in memoir. She concludes that it's part of the contract with the reader to "be an unflinchingly reliable narrator" (27). She also makes a useful distinction between truth in fiction and truth in memoir: "While imagination certainly plays a role in both kinds of writing [memoir and fiction], the application of it in memoir is *circumscribed by the facts*, while in fiction it is *circumscribed by what the reader will believe*" (ibid.).

William Zinsser, in *Inventing the Truth: The Art and Craft of Memoir*, talks about a disagreement he and his mother had about his presentation of his grandmother in his memoir, *Five Boyhoods*. Zinsser says, "The truth is somewhere between my mother's version and mine. But she was like that to *me* and that's the only truth a memoir writer can work with" (12).

Lee Gutkind, in *The Art of Creative Nonfiction: Writing and Selling the Literature of Reality*, agrees that we must work to find the inherent truth of our story but suggests we employ what he calls "expansive thinking," which allows "three-dimensional thought and scenic expression in a novelistic context" (118). We'll explore more tools to excavate "scenic expression" in chapter 4.

It's up to you to define your truth in the particular story you have to tell. Of course, you won't be able to remember dialogue word for word from years ago. But if you create your characters fully, they will speak authentically within your story, and their words and actions will emerge within the context you have established. For further discussion on truth, we refer you to Judith Barrington's and William Zinsser's books. Vivian Gornick's *The Situation and the Story: The Art of Personal Narrative* is also a rich source regarding the nuances of a memoir writer's ethics. Gornick excavates the memoir's value in testifying to one's own particular story and the power of both reader and writer to witness the personal journey.

Part of finding your story will be uncovering the particular self where the story lives. It's this self that will guide you in discovering the truth of your story as well. In chapter 7 we'll revisit this issue from your, the writer's, perspective.

THE OCCASION OF THE TELLING AND ORGANIZING THE MEMOIR

When we decided to talk about ways of organizing the memoir and then started looking at the stacks of books piled on our desks, we realized that there are as many ways to organize the memoir as there are memoirs themselves. That said, the more we looked, the more we realized that the memoirs that resonate most with readers seem to be organized around a distinct catalyst. We'll delve into more specifics of structuring the memoir in chapter 3, but here we'll look at a few effective types of organizations that directly affect the occasion of the telling.

She Died, so I Remember

The first way of approaching the occasion of the telling is via some momentous occasion in the memoirist's "now" that leads him or her back to his or her "then." Here, for example, is the beginning of Patti Smith's National Book Award–winning *Just Kids*: "I was asleep when he died. I had called the hospital to say one more good night, but he had gone under, beneath layers of morphine. I held the receiver and listened to his labored breathing through the phone, knowing I would never hear him again" (xi). Smith's dear friend, the photographer Robert Mapplethorpe, has died, occasioning Patti to go back to the beginning of their lives together. After this opening, Smith circles back to the moment when Patti and Robert's story begins, with the bulk of this memoir told chronologically. As Patti and Robert develop as artists, they are on a trajectory as a pair as well as on unique paths that diverge sharply. The memoir is a record of their friendship, love, and commitment; their artist selves, which could never have existed without each other; and their unique stories.

Other recent memoirs using this approach include Joan Didion's (which we mentioned at the beginning of this chapter); Meghan O'Rourke's *The Long Goodbye*, which explores her mother's death; and Joyce Carol Oates's *A Widow's Tale*, about the death of her husband, Raymond Smith.

And Then, in an Instant, Everything Changed

Another way to approach a memoir's beginning is to *spotlight* the moment when everything in the author's life changed. In this mode of telling, the experiencing narrator thinks her life is on one course when, suddenly and unexpectedly, something intervenes that changes everything. Abigail Thomas does this in *A Three Dog Life*: "Monday, April 24, at nine forty at night, our doorman Pedro called me on the intercom. 'Your dog is in the elevator,' he said. The world had just changed forever, and I think I knew it even then. 'My dog? Where is my husband?' I asked" (11). This harrowing passage spotlights the moment when Abigail and her husband Rich's life together changes irrevocably. Unlike the relatively chronological line that Smith uses after her occasion of the telling, however, Thomas instead follows two narrative threads: what happens *after* this moment and her life with Rich *before* it.

In Jeannette Walls's deservedly popular *The Glass Castle*, the narrator is in a taxi on her way to a party in New York City when she sees her mother rooting through a dumpster. This spotlit moment takes our narrator back into her chaotic childhood with the eccentric family that caused her to struggle while at the same time taught her to love and to think for herself. The occasion of the telling is Walls's realization that her past is a part of her, which leads her to break open the barrier to the life events that brought her to this moment: "It had been months since I laid eyes on Mom, and when she looked up, I was overcome with panic that she'd see me and call out my name, and that someone on the way to the same party would spot us together and Mom would introduce herself and my secret would be out" (3). When Walls and her mother have lunch soon after this spotlit moment, the author asks, "'And what am I supposed to tell people about my parents?' 'Just tell the truth,' Mom said. 'That's simple enough'" (ibid.). And so, on the next page, Walls begins her story.

Now and Then, Then and Now

How you arrange time in a memoir is one of the most important decisions you'll make about its organization, and your decisions about time are directly linked to the occasion of the telling. As an example, in *Heaven's Coast*, Mark Doty revisits the death of his life partner, Wally, from AIDS. Exploring very specific details about Wally's death takes the narrator into the key moments of their lives together as well as into his own journey of going on without Wally.

The remembering narrator fluidly moves back and forth between past events (not chronologically but associatively) and the place where he stands to remember. This style of organization requires great skill, but because Doty is foremost a poet, he is particularly adept at navigating this metaphoric and literal journey. Each scene and internal realization add up to a complicated whole, creating an organic narrative, one that is particularly effective because it mirrors the complexity of its intertwined subjects, life and death. As Doty phrases it in his preface, "This book was written in the flux of change; I wrote it not from a single stillpoint but from the forward momentum of a current of grief. I wanted to allow for shifts in my perspective as time moved forward, as what we think of as healing began. What is healing, but a shift in perspective?" (ix).

SPOTLIGHT EXERCISE

Writing: Using the notes you made in the spotlight exercise about family stories earlier in this chapter, take one story you remember and play with its organization in time. Try to come up with three versions of how it could be told. For example, if the story were told by an older sibling, how might it begin? How might the speaker go from now to then and back? Another example is noting how the story's time sense would change if three or four members of the family chimed in to tell the story. Each might start events in a different place and give the listener a different context.

The challenge of structuring time and the movement between *now* and *then* involve the two yous and will be explored in more depth in the next chapter.

As one you is the remembering narrator and the other you is the experiencing one, the movement between the two determines the rhythm of time in your memoir.

CONSEQUENCE AND THE
OCCASION OF THE TELLING

The decision to embark on a memoir comes most often from a make-or-break time or event in the author's life long after the events about which she or he writes have taken place. Speaking out about this difficult time is risky and life-changing, but, as readers, we're drawn to memoirs that explore how others face life's greatest challenges—we want to learn, in a sense, how to navigate our own lives. While critics sometimes dismiss memoirs as records of trauma and dysfunction, the fact is that few lives are free of either. We read memoirs to share in the personal stories of others, stories that resonate with our own.

If you write your memoir about an occasion that has a charge for you and you're invested in the consequence of your story, then your readers will be invested, too. Your occasion of the telling telegraphs this sense of risk and consequence from the very beginning of your memoir.

FURTHER SPOTLIGHT EXERCISES

Reading: Compare the occasion of the telling in two of the memoirs from the bibliography or from books of your choice. Are you committed to read further after reading the writer's occasion? Why or why not?

Writing: List five events in your life that are significant. Maybe they involve specific people or a move from one place to another. Maybe they spotlight other transitions, or possibly they are key turning points that haunt you. Don't think too much; just write them down.

Taking each of the five events from the previous paragraph, imagine a photograph that captures some essence of the event. Write down a detailed description of what is in that photograph. What is in the foreground? What is in the background? What (or who) is not in the photograph, even though you know that person or thing should be a part of it? Who might have taken the photograph, if it were real?

Now choose one of the images from the above paragraph and make it move. Begin to construct a scene around that moving photograph. What happens because of what event or person? Again, don't think too much; just try to get down this key moment in as much detail as you can.

One consequence that we sometimes don't anticipate but that nonetheless is often the case is that we ourselves will be changed by writing about the past. The act of translating our experience into the hard reality of the written word makes us see ourselves differently. It broadens our perspective and yet focuses it as well. As if we're using a magnifying glass, new details will emerge and take their place within the larger picture.

The act of writing itself is risky, but so is daring to face the past and dive into its clutter and layers of truth. Perhaps the biggest consequence of finding the occasion of the telling is to assert that our lives matter. We all have many stories, and each story is part of the larger story of our families and the communities in which we live. It takes courage to claim our stories, and yet sharing them is an act of enormous generosity, because, in doing so, we allow others to learn from our experience as much as we individually learn from it in the writing.

The image you create in the above writing exercise or from any one of the five events you noted may evolve into your occasion of the telling. Each of these moments has consequence (you've remembered it all this time); each changed your life in some significant way. Spotlit moments like these are the seeds of memoir, the images that reveal us to ourselves.

As we move through *Find Your Story*, we'll ask you to pause and reflect about your own story, to write down some of the images and thoughts and insights that will shape your narrative. By the time you finish this book, you will most likely have a blueprint for creating a memoir. Possibly, you'll have the seeds for several separate pieces or books. What's most important, though, is that you'll have taken the leap to committing to write. Through the process of sifting and examining your impressions and memories, the act of writing will become a familiar one, a process you'll look forward to rather than one that feels out of reach or too difficult to attempt.

In the next chapter, we'll explore more fully the two yous and finding a place to stand, which are intertwined with each story's consequence for its writer. A story's place to stand spotlights the moment where you must begin to share your story and is returned to again and again. We'll examine how this remembering self serves as both reflector and witness, key elements in the memoir's process of discovery.

2

The Two Yous

Finding a Place to Stand

Life is not what one has lived but what one remembers and how one
remembers it in order to recount it.

—GABRIEL GARCÍA MÁRQUEZ, *Vivir para contarla*
(*Living to Tell the Tale*)

As we continue to seek the occasion of the telling that prompts any memoir—
the *why* of our story—we are led to examine the speaker and *how* a particular
story can be told. A memoir is told by an author in the present (the *remembering self*) who takes the reader to various stages of his or her past (the *experiencing self*). The journey of this past self—along with its lessons and conflicts—
gives the story its tension and informs the author in the present. Because of
the dual nature of memoir, your story is a journey of self-discovery not only
for you, its author, but for the reader as well.

The *remembering self* refers to the author in the present.

The *experiencing self* refers to the author in the past.

As Sue William Silverman notes in *Fearless Confessions: A Writer's Guide to
Memoir*, "A memoir . . . is only partially about writing recollected facts of what
happened. The other part requires a more authorial observation and understanding of events . . . written through the viewpoint—and with the insight—
of the author sitting at her or his desk *trying to figure out what it all means*"
(8, emphasis added). Thus, remembering what happened, and reflecting on it,
allows you to act as a witness to your own story.

It's our belief that this witnessing is an important reason for memoir's
current popularity. As Vivian Gornick notes in *The Situation and the Story*,
"The age is characterized by a need to testify. Everywhere in the world women

and men are rising up to tell their story out of the now commonly held belief that one's own life signifies" (91). Memoir matters because it's in coming to understand individual stories that we find our commonality.

In this chapter, we'll explore the challenges and pleasures of this duality and suggest strategies for walking the tightrope between the two yous.

THE REMEMBERING SELF

"To write one's life is to live it twice," Patricia Hampl notes in *I Could Tell You Stories: Sojourns in the Land of Memory*, "and the second living is both spiritual and historical, for a memoir reaches deep within the personality as it seeks its narrative form" (37). Your reminiscent narrator grounds your story in its present, anchoring the moment of departure back into the story for both you and your reader. We call these two selves—aspects of yourself at different times—the *two yous*, as it's useful for the purposes of creating the story to separate the you who remembers, who has gained perspective and insight during the intervening years since the memoir's events, from the you who has lived through their dramatic arc.

It may be helpful for you to think of the remembering narrator as the you who says, "If only I'd known then what I know now," or the you who tells us, "Let me take you back to the way my life was then." An example of this you, who takes us on a journey into her past, can be found in Annie Dillard's iconic memoir, *An American Childhood*, when she begins her prologue: "When everything else has gone from my brain—the President's name, the state capitals, the neighborhoods where I lived, and then my own name and what it was on earth I sought, and then at length the faces of my friends, and finally the faces of my family—when all this has dissolved, what will be left, I believe, is topology: the dreaming memory of land as it lay this way and that" (3).

Dillard provides us here with an arresting occasion of the telling ("the dreaming memory" of the land of her past) while at the same time signaling to the reader that she will *mediate* her history, and its landscapes, through her remembering self, thus following Patricia Hampl's suggestion that "[m]emoir is the intersection of narration and reflection, of storytelling and essay writing. It can present its story *and* consider the meaning of the story" (*I Could Tell*, 33). Dillard's beginning also alerts us to the lyrical tone and ruminative qualities of her voice, an aspect of memoir we'll be covering in more detail in chapter 6.

Just as the occasion of the telling offers you a place to stand, employing a remembering self gives you a place to view the self, allowing you objective distance from what is ordinarily subjective and habitual. Empowering the you who looks back at your past offers a vehicle for tackling the hard work of revisiting your past.

In Mark Doty's *Heaven's Coast*, the remembering self we've come to rely on throughout is well positioned to offer this passage near the end of the book: "What was can't be restored; I can neither have Wally back in the flesh, nor return to the self I inhabited before his death. The vessel's not cracked but broken, all the way through, permanently. The break, from now on, is an inescapable part of who I am, perhaps *the* inescapable part. Hasn't it become my essential definition, my central fact: I loved a man who died?" (286).

By this time in the memoir, the reader has traveled with Doty from the first positive diagnosis of Wally's HIV through to his death. Doty, and the reader, concurrently move forward into a life now characterized by Wally's absence. This journey hasn't been chronological, but nonetheless, throughout the book, the tension in the story reverberates between the remembering self, who knows his partner is gone, and the experiencing self, who in the past experiences one loss after another until Wally's death actually occurs. The experiencing self is too busy reacting to have the perspective the remembering self offers.

In this sense, the remembering self is a comforting presence. By grounding this narrator (or, in some cases, by surviving to write the story at all), you, like Doty, assure the reader that you've made it through the difficult journey that many memoirs map. Of course, as Doty so eloquently notes above, you're not the same as you were before the events in the book took place; you've changed profoundly. The dialogue between the two yous showcases that transformation by documenting its journey in rising and falling action, climactic moments, and resolution.

THE EXPERIENCING SELF

Because stories are most engrossing when the reader can experience their events through sensory details, your task as a memoirist is to show the stages of your change with scenes that bring the past alive. In these scenes, the experiencing self holds sway—the you who lacks the insight distance brings, the you who acts and reacts *in the moment*.

This other, experiencing self is vividly shown in Koren Zailckas's *Fury: A Memoir*, when the protagonist is addressed by a man seated next to her on an international flight when she doesn't feel like talking—something most of us have experienced at one time or another. In this passage, however, Zailckas takes the familiar experience much further, going back and forth between her experiencing self and the remembering self. She begins with the former, as she says to the man: "'I don't mean to be rude, but a man just broke up with me in the worst way, at the worst possible time, and under the worst possible circumstances in my limited experience, so you'll have to excuse me if I don't feel like talking.' . . . But the old man doesn't seem to have heard me. He describes the sights he saw in London" (7–8). At this point, the remembering self, the grounding narrator, breaks in with a comment that reveals her distance from the self in the past: "If I had an ounce of attention for anything outside of my own suffering, I would have cracked a neighborly smile by now. But in this black hole, no human warmth can reach me" (8).

Notice how the back and forth of the two yous appears effortless here. This ease of moving in time is one of your goals as a memoir writer, as then the reader not only learns quickly to make these time shifts but ceases to realize that they're even on the page. Because Zailckas negotiates the dance between her two narrators so skillfully in this scene, the reader feels the tension of knowing what the narrator *wishes* she had done while at the same time braces for what she'll *do*, which, ultimately, is to explode into anger.

In such a scene, the remembering self and the experiencing self appear far apart: the remembering self, with her acquired wisdom, would truly have behaved differently, as we've noted. The distance between the two yous in this case may bring to mind the film *Sliding Doors* with Gwyneth Paltrow, in which one version of her character chooses one trajectory through life and another takes a completely different path.

SPOTLIGHT EXERCISE

Writing: "A memoirist gazes at a canvas that's already swirling with color," Sue William Silverman writes in *Fearless Confessions*. "Where a fiction writer crafts images onto that blank canvas, the memoirist decides what to remove from it" (31).

Consider the canvas of a scene from your past you'd like to re-create on paper as if it were a still life. Now take a further step back and consider yourself considering that scene. Observe the observer you. What does she see now that she didn't see then? What does she think about what she's observing? Without judging either of the two yous, make some notes about the remembering you studying the experiencing you.

As the sequence above happens early in the first chapter, it also dramatizes Zailckas's occasion of the telling—the incendiary anger that characterizes the protagonist at this stage of her life. (You'll recall that the title of this memoir is *Fury*.) As a result, the author combines two important tools of the memoir writer—to explosive effect.

THE DANCE OF THE TWO YOUS

Whether or not they're aware of how it's being negotiated, readers of memoir are drawn to the back-and-forth perspective on life's challenges offered by the two yous. But creating the two yous requires contemplation as well as digging deep into the past. While it's easier to sketch the past, to make lists of events that happened, than to present the stories of our lives *fully digested*, so that both reader and writer apprehend the experience in a nuanced way, it's the back and forth that creates memorable memoirs.

Another way of looking at it is that, in moving between the two yous, you the writer don't just mine your memories; you refine them as well. As memoir writers, we gain perspective on our lives by *re*immersing ourselves in the messy details through the process of writing them down. As Patricia Hampl notes, "We embody, if unwittingly and impartially, our history, even our prehistory. The past courses through our veins. The self is the instrument which allows us not only to live this truth but to contemplate it, and thereby to be comforted by meaning" (*I Could Tell*, 97).

Still, it's one thing to journal, to, as Natalie Goldberg puts it, "write down the bones." It's quite another to reshape your material into a *journey* readers eagerly join. Consider how you as a reader might experience Mary Karr's journey through her unusual childhood in *The Liars' Club* without the wise-cracking—and wise—voice of the reminiscent adult Karr telling us, "My sharpest memory is of a single instant surrounded by dark" (3). After beginning here, with her reminiscent narrator, Karr immediately moves back into the memory itself: "I was seven, and our family doctor knelt before me where I sat on the mattress on the bare floor. He wore a yellow golf shirt unbuttoned so that sprouts of hair showed in a V shape on his chest" (ibid.).

Having established her two selves in the opening paragraph, Karr masterfully moves back and forth between them throughout her award-winning memoir. The dialogue between these two selves allows the reader to discover insights that move the story forward via an interplay between Karr's two yous. Thus, the act of looking back allows you, the writer, to gather the most salient and striking details of your past and mine them for a heightened realization.

While it's something of a truism to say that those who forget history are doomed to repeat it, by writing your way through a complex experience, as

Karr does, by weaving the past series of yous with your present, remembering self, you can also discover a way to move on from that experience—to not, in other words, repeat it. "The writing process itself is part of the journey," Sue William Silverman notes. "The insights you have while writing aren't things you knew at the time the events happened. It's only through writing about events after they happened—as we craft our memoirs—that we come to understand what they mean" (45). Part of the pleasure of writing memoir lies in achieving these deeper realizations.

The Power of Testifying

Just as testifying—retelling—experience helps us process it and then move on, the conversation between the two yous enables you to assess the past, learn from it, and share it with others. A striking example can be found in Elizabeth Gilbert's best-selling memoir *Eat, Pray, Love*. One of the many reasons for this book's success was the sense of community it forged among its readers. Through reading Gilbert's book and talking about it, readers felt that their similar yearnings for experience (including travel to exotic places) and understanding had been witnessed.

SPOTLIGHT EXERCISE

Reading: Choose a passage from a memoir you admire (you may wish to choose one we've mentioned in this chapter) where you notice the narrator shifting between the two yous. What perspective(s) does this movement in time provide toward your understanding the protagonist more deeply? Are there gaps between the narrator's assessment of the events in this passage and what you perceive as a reader? Often the reader makes connections that the writer may not consciously have intended. It's through these connections that author and reader witness each other and that the reader gains new understanding.

Although a very different book in tone and structure, Joan Didion's *The Year of Magical Thinking* similarly bears witness for a large audience through its meditation on the sudden loss of a dear one. The most memorable memoirs serve this testimonial function through both the two yous within the book and the connection of book to audience. The ability to create intimacy and community at the same time helps explain the popularity and the significance of memoirs like Gilbert's and Didion's.

"The truth that memoir has to offer is not neatly opposite from fiction's truth," writes Patricia Hampl. "Its method and habits are different, and it is perhaps a more perverse genre than the novel: It *seems* to be about an individual self, but it is revealed as a minion of memory which belongs not only to the personal world but to the public realm" (*I Could Tell*, 205). This shared experience between writer and communities of readers gives the memoir its power as a genre.

Taking Yourself by the Hand

Often when we begin writing, we really don't know where we're going. We just know we feel compelled to write about our experience to try to understand it. In *Ron Carlson Writes a Story*, Carlson describes how the story itself finds its own way: "Beginning a story without knowing all the terrain is not a comfortable feeling. . . . But there are moments in the process of writing a story when you must tolerate that feeling: you stay alert to everything that is happening and by listening and watching, *you find out where you are going by going there*" (15, emphasis added).

One of the ways we find our way through the terrain that Carlson speaks of when writing memoir is through the back and forth of the two yous. When we decide to write about something—whether a difficult move in childhood, the death of someone close to us, negotiating our way through an illness, the process of growing up itself—we don't know where that writing process will take us. In fact, even though we're writing about the past, we often don't yet know the end of the story we need to tell. What Carlson reminds us is that, by excavating the past through the prism of the present, we will eventually find our way.

Excavation is key to this process. It's also the most difficult part. You may think that you're finally ready to tell that difficult story, but you may discover that, when you at last have the time to write, you'll do *anything*—from the dishes to your tax return—to avoid returning to those emotionally fraught memories on the page. As Carlson puts it, "All the valuable writing I've done in the last ten years has been done in the first twenty minutes after the first time I've wanted to leave the room" (15).

Robert Olen Butler's *From Where You Dream* explores this difficulty in great depth, suggesting that it's only in digging deep that we will find what really matters to our story: "When you write, you cannot flinch. You have to go down into that deepest, darkest, most roiling, white-hot place. . . . Whatever scared the hell out of you down there . . . you have to go down there; down into the deepest part of it, and you can't flinch, can't walk away. That's the only way to create a work of art—even though you have plenty of defense mechanisms to keep you out of there" (18).

What comes up from this "white-hot place" will be the pure, raw emotion of your story. You won't be able to spend a long time there, and you'll later want to revisit the material with your remembering narrator along to turn the raw emotion into art. "Trust memories," writes Sue William Silverman. "Trust feelings. Write *your* truth, how *you* remember events. Writing, in fact, will bring you *closer* to your truth" (130). Learning to move between the two yous will help you temper the raw emotion necessary for reader identification with the steady hand of the older but wiser person you've become.

SPOTLIGHT EXERCISE

Reading: During the Middle Ages, alchemists sought to turn lesser elements into gold. While their experiments couldn't succeed, as a writer you possess the tools to, as we note above, "turn raw emotion into art." The first of these tools, of course, is the memories themselves. But negotiating this territory requires a willingness to mine, and then refine, your work.

   Find a passage in a memoir you've read where the author has clearly gone somewhere difficult. How does he use his two yous to negotiate this territory? What would be missing if the remembering narrator weren't there? Employing a remembering narrator to witness his difficult return can be a key to negotiating it.

Negotiating Duality

Moving seamlessly between your two narrators is a skill you'll come to refine in your own way only over time. The process requires thought and revision; the analogy that comes to mind when we teach is that negotiating this territory can be similar to tiptoeing through a minefield. The good news is that, in this case, practice makes a big difference. The internal logic of your story, through time, will also at some point take over and make this negotiation somewhat instinctive.

One of the side benefits of employing the two yous is that it can offer others in your story the opportunity to give their different take on the proceedings. Let's say, for example, that your memory of an important moment from your childhood is entirely different from a sibling's recollection. In *The Liars' Club*, Mary Karr negotiates this territory by parenthetically adding her sister

Lecia's voice to her own at these moments: "(If I gave my big sister a paragraph here, she would correct my memory. To this day, she claims that she genuinely mourned for the old lady, who was a kindly soul, and that I was too little and mean-spirited then to remember things right . . .)" (47).

Unlike Karr, Mark Doty relies on only his own memories. But Doty negotiates his duality first by acknowledging it and second by exploring it and its meaning. Near the end of *Heaven's Coast*, for example, Doty meets a coyote in the dunes. Stunned, he decides that Wally has sent him: "This apparition, my—ghost, was it? spirit animal? real creature carrying the presence of my love? Perhaps it doesn't matter. I've never seen one in the middle of the day before or since, and never been so frankly studied from the other side of wildness, from a world I cannot enter" (304).

The decision about how to acknowledge the subjectivity of memory is one that you will want to consider as you write—and rewrite—your own story. These two examples are but two ways of negotiating this territory. We'll look in greater detail at considering—and including—others' memories and points of view in chapter 7.

Sensory Cues as Keys to Memory

One simple way to move around in time is to use your remembering or experiencing narrator's *sensory cues*. But while contemporary Westerners rely mostly on seeing and hearing, the most vital and direct sensory cues utilize the limbic senses: smell, taste, and touch.

Sensory cues employ a scent, taste, or touch to trigger a flashback.

Consider, for example, a smell from your childhood, whether it's Aunt Maudie's face powder or the lingering scent of marijuana emanating from under your brother's bedroom door. A mere whiff of this scent and you are transported back to the moment you first smelled it as if you're once again in that moment. Sight and sound alone can't trip this time travel. Only our oldest senses, the ones tied to our ancestors' survival mechanisms, kick in this way.

What this means for you the memoirist is that you can use a sensory cue to instantly transport both your narrator and your reader to a moment in your narrator's past. In the following excerpt from *The Glass Castle*, Jeannette Walls describes setting herself on fire while cooking hotdogs at the age of three. Here touch, sound, and sight magnify her pain and distress: "I felt a blaze of heat on my right side. . . . Frozen with fear, I watched the yellow-white flames make a ragged brown line up the pink fabric of my skirt and climb my stomach. . . . I screamed. I smelled the burning and heard a horrible crackling as the fire singed my hair and eyelashes" (9).

Walls confides to the reader that this is her first memory, reinforcing our sense of when her experiencing self begins in time. But in addition, this moment allows us to bear witness as readers to the enormous leap Walls has made in her life from this terrified little girl to the sophisticated and accomplished woman who discovers her mother digging in a Manhattan dumpster many years later.

Note, too, how the sensory details Walls chooses enhance reader identification with her experiencing self. It's of course unlikely that you have ever set yourself on fire, but the vivid image of the flames climbing up the little girl's skirt, coupled with the sound and smell of the fire, create a horrifyingly real scene. We'll go into even greater depth about how the right details can bring your memoir to life in chapter 5.

Using Language and Imagery
to Move between the Two Yous

Another way of moving back and forth between the two yous is via the language you use. After all, your experiencing self is in the past, a place you've moved on from, and so you will likely speak in a slightly different way both in dialogue and in your ability to analyze or describe. Here, for example, is Mary Karr negotiating the balance beam between her young self and the memoirist: "I guess I concentrated so hard on Gordon that day, because I almost couldn't bear to look at Mother. She'd become the picture of somebody nuts. For one thing, she'd tried to dye her hair red that fall, but wound up with a substance less hair than pelt. It was the overall color and texture of dried alfalfa" (223).

Because of the everyday diction Karr uses, unless one looks closely at her use of language, it's easy to miss the way she employs it to move between her experiencing and remembering selves. If one weren't reading as a writer, in fact, one might argue that there is no difference between the two. But only a remembering adult narrator could come up with phrasings like "less hair than pelt" and "the overall color and texture of dried alfalfa." Karr's language may be disguised by the spice she adds, but in truth it's one more tool she employs to marvelous effect.

A repeated image or sequence can also transport the reader between the remembering self and the experiencing one. In *The Year of Magical Thinking*, Joan Didion returns over and over again to her memory of serving her husband a second Scotch before dinner. At that moment John was alive, and yet in the next he was not. Didion's inability to grasp that moment takes us back to her occasion of the telling when we stand with the experiencing self who herself stands helplessly by as the paramedics storm her home.

SPOTLIGHT EXERCISE

Writing: In conversation, we seldom pay attention to the way we use language. There may be moments when we choose our words more carefully—when we need to get a point across, or when we're disagreeing with someone about whom we care deeply—but most of us use our own particular everyday diction to express what we wish to share with others verbally.

How we express ourselves in writing, however, involves a more elevated diction or, put another way, a selection and reordering of words and phrases to convey meaning on the page. When we add the two yous to this equation, it becomes all the more challenging a prospect.

For this exercise, select a moment from your past that you hope to include in your memoir. First, write the scene as you remember it, using words and the writing skill you possess now, as a remembering narrator.

When you've finished this scene, put it away. Now write the same scene as if you were once again that younger you. Nothing you've learned since that moment can enter into this writing—not words, not experience, not hindsight. Try to use active verbs that bring to life the emotions you were experiencing then, and don't forget to include more than just visual senses—add sounds, scents, tastes, feelings.

After finishing the second scene, read the two versions. Chances are, there will be parts of each of them that will work very well for your memoir. If you want to take this exercise one step further, try moving back and forth between these two yous to interweave these two renditions into one scene containing both your voices.

You may also choose to use the life of the mind to move from your reminiscent narrator into a moment in the past. Annie Dillard does this repeatedly in *An American Childhood*: "When I was five . . . I would not go to bed willingly because something came into my room. This was a private matter between me and it. If I spoke of it, it would kill me. Who could breathe as this thing searched for me over the very corners of the room? Who could ever breathe freely again? I lay in the dark" (20).

Notice how by using both her remembering and experiencing narrators, Dillard can comment on the irrationality of her childhood fear while at the same time acknowledging its importance. Like a dance, moving between the two yous involves practiced steps as well as improvisation once you've mastered those steps.

THE NATURE OF MEMORY

Recent research confirms what many of us have long suspected: memory is fallible, subject not only to our own, well, subjectiveness but also to the vagaries of time. In chapter 1 we looked at some of the challenges concerning memory and truth, and we'll consider the ethics of writing your story in chapter 7.

Consider a spotlit moment from your childhood at which everyone in your immediate family was present—a meal, say, or a car ride. Chances are, if you were to say to your brother or sister, "Remember that time Dad swerved to avoid the snake in the road and hit the Joneses' oak tree?," he or she might reply, "It wasn't a snake" or "It was the Smiths' spruce."

The thing about memoir is that each of your versions of this memory is valid. If your sibling were to write about it, it would of course be a different story. In the end, there are as many different versions of something that was not recorded verbatim as there were people present—each true to its rememberer. *You* are writing *your* memoir. So be true to yourself—both of

---

FURTHER SPOTLIGHT EXERCISES

Writing: Choosing a memory from an exercise in chapter 1 or another memory that occurs to you right now, write a few paragraphs establishing the you who is remembering now, looking back on yourself in the past. Move back and forth between what you recall and how you view the incident/experience/action now. The insights you are able to bring to bear on the past as you do this illustrate the power of the remembering self and your ability to frame your experience with a depth the experiencing self cannot access.

Reading: Now read what you have written and answer the following questions: What are several possibilities for where to stand in recounting this particular memory? Is there one place that feels compelling to you? Why?

you. You'll find as you write that your own recollections continue to undergo revision. In that light, the two yous offer a way to show the discrepancies between the experiencing narrator's point of view and the you who is writing the story now.

Vivian Gornick reminds us: "Truth in a memoir is achieved not through a recital of actual events; it is achieved when the reader comes to believe that the writer is working hard to *engage* with the experience at hand" (91, emphasis added). It's this engagement of your two yous that will lead you to your own particular truth.

❡

As you begin to explore your story, you may use one or some combination of the above methods of moving between the two yous. Or, as you discover your voice and your story, you may come up with your own distinctive approach.

Our next chapter focuses on ways to build your memoir, exploring different structures and ways of arranging a story to heighten its effect. Structure not only organizes your text episodically but also provides *scaffolding* that supports the plot and meaning from within. Structure is to story what the skeleton is to our bodies. Without it, all is formless, and nothing moves forward. In chapter 3 we'll look at specific tools to help you find the structure that enhances your unique narrative.

3

Building a Narrative

Laying Down the Bones

Structure isn't a prefabricated box you cram your story into. It is a
flexible framework that helps you move through your narrative without
losing your way.

> —NANCY LAMB, *The Art and Craft of Storytelling: A Comprehensive
> Guide to Classic Writing Techniques*

We humans know innately that good stories have a sequence of action that
dramatically leads readers (or listeners) from an opening situation (the occasion of the telling) into a conflict that ultimately has a climax and a resolution.
This arrangement of interrelated events is what is called a story's *plot*.

Plot is the dramatic sequencing of *events* in your story.

No matter how natural happenings may seem on the page, plot and the
actions that make it up are always carefully devised and crafted by the writer.
Organizing events into a sequence is an essential component of storytelling,
something we all do naturally from the time when we're very young. We tell
stories about ourselves, our friends, and our family members, and, if we're
writers, we write them down. Common plots are often repeated—in mysteries, for example, one person wants to get rid of another person and enlists a
third person to help. Many memoirs take the protagonist on a hero's journey
from a difficult childhood to a productive adulthood. What makes a plot particular is the way it's *structured*, the way the sequence of events is presented
to the reader.

Structure is the *framework* that contains your story
(and includes plot).

Plot and structure differ distinctly and yet work in tandem to give your story its essential texture. Plot has a mechanical aspect, as the narrative has to move forward from its beginning to its end: action rises and falls, and characters' motives play out through the dance of conflict and motivation. We'll explore the workings of plot through scene in chapter 4, where you'll learn how to build the separate blocks that combine to form the plot of your story.

In this chapter we'll look at structure as the *container* for the mode and arrangement of the telling that organically allows events to create impact and meaning. While the events in your memoir may share commonalities with others, the *form* it takes—including decisions about time frames, audience/ reader, and ways of telling—is unique and transforms what might have been routine into a standout narrative.

The occasion of the telling is a place to begin observing the interdependence of plot and structure, so we'll begin our discussion by exploring how the occasion initiates and provides perspective on action.

BEGINNING YOUR STORY

Memory can act as a sorting device. When something stands out, it's usually for a reason. Such memories (or, as Lisa Dale Norton calls them, "shimmering images") act as your story's *catalyst*, a precipitating action that sets its world in motion. Most often, the catalyst of the story is referenced in the occasion of the telling, which we discussed in chapter 1.

A story's *catalyst* is a specific incident that illuminates the occasion of the telling and sets the story in motion.

In the first chapter of Koren Zailckas's book *Fury*, the catalyzing incident that motivates her story is her rage at a fellow passenger on an international flight who keeps talking to her even after she has signaled that she wishes to be silent. Zailckas finally erupts in a tirade that plunges the cabin into shocked silence until a baby wakes and begins to howl. The catalyst, in this case an example of the protagonist's quickly provoked rage, very specifically motivates the ensuing story and illustrates the occasion of the telling.

In Linda Gray Sexton's memoir *Searching for Mercy Street: My Journey Back to My Mother, Anne Sexton*, the occasion of the telling and the catalyst are even more closely linked. This memoir details a daughter's struggle to come to terms with her mother's suicide, which is clear from the first page of the book.

The epigraph for the first chapter, "The Letter," is an Anne Sexton poem called "Suicide Note":

> I will go now
> without old age or disease,
> wildly but accurately,
> knowing my best route. (3)

This epigraph dramatically points to two things: (1) the eloquent presence of Anne Sexton will shadow every page of this memoir; and (2) her premature leave-taking prompts the daughter's search that leads to the memoir itself. Notice how few words it takes to do this—the strongest writing is both succinct and resonant of the book's major themes. The first words of your story establish your subject and introduce your reader to why your narrator and your story matter.

Following this epigraph, Linda Gray Sexton describes finding a letter from her mother that she immediately thinks could be the suicide note that she has long sought. In this instance, the occasion of the telling—the discovery of a long-misplaced letter from her mother—combines with the catalyst that sets the plot in motion.

SPOTLIGHT EXERCISE

Writing: Let's pause for a moment to consider how you might apply a catalyst to your own memoir. Take some time now to select one of the occasions of the telling you recorded at the end of chapter 1. Next, write down one or more catalysts that could trigger a specific first scene in your memoir. Don't censor; write down whatever first comes to you. While these events may not begin your memoir, they may very well be clues to other chapters or significant scenes in the narrative.

Catalysts and Conflicts

While it's unlikely that your mother was a world-renowned poet, and so you won't have a snippet of a poem to work epigrammatically, as Sexton does, the occasion of the telling you discovered in chapter 1 nonetheless will provide an entrance and a catalyst that lead you—and your reader—into your story. That's because dynamic catalysts inevitably lead to *conflict*. Life doesn't proceed effortlessly—obstacles get in the way of the most well-planned existence—and neither do stories.

Conflict occurs when someone wants something that he or she
doesn't get or when a character is blocked.

Mapping the Tension

As we've noted, many memoirs are about the blockages that occur in childhood as well as in marriages, in careers, and/or with health. From the earliest recorded memoirs, the genre has provided a vehicle for self-discovery
and reflection. The plot in memoir therefore inevitably moves from a state of
incoherence, lack, or confusion into growth.

In the case of Linda Gray Sexton, the letter from her mother (which turns
out not to be a suicide note at all but a letter Sexton wrote to her daughter
years before her death) is one of many obstacles to tracing her own emotional
history. The poet's unpredictable behavior—swinging between tender attention and bursts of rage—continually plunges the daughter's sense of safety
and security into doubt during her childhood. Her mother is both beloved
subject and source of conflict. This tension repeatedly creates barriers to Linda
Gray Sexton's maturation.

Sexton begins chapter 2, "In Exile," with the following: "My story as a
daughter and my mother's story as a mother begins in a Boston suburb, back
in the 1950s, when I was exiled from my childhood home to make room for
someone else: Mother's mental illness, which lived among us like a fifth person" (11). Throughout this memoir, the writer uses her mother's poetic gift as
"evidence" of both her genius and her precarious mental state. Anne Sexton's
poems are thus woven into the narrative just as her moods and behavior
shaped her daughter's perceptions. The occasion of the telling and the catalyst
for the memoir combine in the mother's words.

In Tobias Wolff's award-winning memoir *This Boy's Life*, the opening words
are: "Our car boiled over again just after my mother and I crossed the Conti-
nental Divide." While Wolff and his mother wait for the engine to cool, a truck
careens past them. "'Oh, Toby,' my mother said, 'he's lost his brakes'" (3). The
stalled car and out-of-control truck are both metaphors for the mother and
son's wandering life. Fleeing from a man she doesn't trust, the mother too has
lost her brakes, and the two drift in the following pages through Utah and on
to Seattle in search of a more stable life.

While in this memoir the occasion marks a moment of standing still, the
racing truck on its way to crash over the guardrail strikes an ominous note for
the reader. We know there are crashes to come for these two characters, that

the time spent waiting for the boiling radiator to cool is brief. The juxtaposition of these two events catalyzes the narrative, setting up the pattern of
stalling out and then running. The mother's remarriage in Seattle to an abu-
sive husband appears to stop this pattern, yet the experiencing narrator must
distance himself from both of these people to find the space to grow up. Taking control of his life remains Wolff's task, which the opening of the memoir
previews.

As these examples reveal, the central issues of your story, including the
main conflicts, determine structural considerations. To help you see how this
works, we'll look at six common structures in detail.

EXAMPLES OF STRUCTURES

As we explore some of the ways memoirs might be structured, please keep in
mind that the structural labels we've applied to various works are not exact;
many books are combinations of different approaches, which we'll point out
as we go along. Think of structure as a sturdy surround that contains narrative bits of different sizes and shapes—as a tough sac that holds and smoothes
the bumpy edges of narrative. As we proceed, we'll also point out some of the
advantages and limitations of each structure in the context of our examples.

Many memoirs begin with a preface or introduction in the remembering
narrator's voice. This allows the reader to learn the occasion of the telling, to
discover why this story is being revisited now. After this preface, the structure
of the larger work will emerge. An example is *The Glass Castle*, in which, after
an opening closer to the narrator's present, the structure reverts to a chronological one, starting with the narrator's childhood and ending at a time closer
to that of the beginning. It may be helpful to think of a *preface* as a way for
the remembering narrator to introduce the experiencing narrator.

A memoir's *preface* often connects the two yous.

Chronological Structure

As with *The Glass Castle*, Patti Smith's *Just Kids* opens with a remembering
narrator who establishes the occasion of the telling. Smith begins with her
dear friend Robert Mapplethorpe's death, the catalyst for her story. After this
sad and lyrical opening, Smith goes back to her own birth in 1946 and early
childhood, along the way establishing that Robert also was born in that year.

In this way, she connects the "just kids" of the title even before they knew each other.

As the book is both a testament to a friendship as well as a history of a time, the chronological structure—moving primarily from the friends' meeting in 1967 until Mapplethorpe's death in 1989—serves Smith well. Structure should always support meaning, and, in this case, the chronological structure serves the book's larger meaning.

With that in mind, it's useful to look at what Smith and her book gain from the structure she chooses. One of her motives in writing the book was to show how she and Robert supported each other emotionally and artistically through late adolescence into adulthood: "I told him that I would continue our work, our collaboration, for as long as I lived. Will you write our story? Do you want me to? You have to he said no one but you can write it. I will do it, I promised" (287). Smith constructs her tale so that we see these near twin spirits intertwining around each other, through time as well as space, from the moment of their meeting. By the end of the book, the reader feels that their meeting was preordained: Patti Smith could not have become the artist she became, nor Robert Mapplethorpe a photographer of renown, without their connection. The chronological structure reinforces both this necessity and their magic together. *Structure* should always reinforce *meaning*.

Along with determining what the writer gains from a chronological structure, we also want to posit some of the limitations such a straightforward structure can impose. Following a strictly linear time line can limit the interaction of the two yous that is so important to a resonant memoir. If the reader is in each moment with the narrator, imagining the future (even if it's known, as it is in a book about celebrities, like *Just Kids*) can feel out of place.

In the case of *Just Kids*, however, the preface and an extended group of poems and photos that form the epilogue have provided Smith a grand palette, one with ample space in which to explore her subjects. She doesn't let her roughly linear time frame limit her; rather, she uses it to let the reader peer into the funhouse mirror of a storied time in art and rock-and-roll history.

SPOTLIGHT EXERCISE

Writing: Because we experience time sequentially, a chronological structure is a good one to try out first. Beginning with the catalyst that you noted earlier in this chapter, list in chronological order what will happen in your memoir.

Circular Structure

In *The Year of Magical Thinking*, Joan Didion's subject is her response to her husband's death, and her plot is the sequence of events she undergoes: first, the death of her husband as she's preparing dinner; next, her immediate re-action of calling an ambulance, witnessing the EMTs' arrival, going to the hospital, and so on. But, rather than proceeding chronologically, as the examples above do, Didion's book moves forward and backward not only through this year of magical thinking, a time when Didion not only tries to trick time into returning her husband but also deals with the severe illness of her adult only child, but also through their life together and her imaginings of what's next—the future. Didion thus employs a circular structure to weave her memoir into a cohesive whole, returning repeatedly to the moment when everything changed, making it her memoir's *anchor*.

In a *circular structure*, a key or catalyzing incident serves as an *anchor* for the story; the narrator returns to it again and again.

Because John's death has changed everything, Didion must return over and over again to the opening image of life changing in a moment, of the two of them talking as she fixes his drink and then his dying, before she can go forward into new events. Similar to a walker in the Chartres labyrinth, Didion can follow other paths, but eventually they lead her back to the center, to the instigating event that catalyzed her journey.

The advantages of circularity in this book are many. First, the structure underscores Didion's struggle to comprehend her husband's death. Often, when we are shocked, we keep going back to the moment when everything changed. In Didion's case, she repeatedly circles back to the occasion of the telling, the sudden death itself.

Second, this structure forces the reader to experience Didion's psycholog-ical reality with her by returning to key images, compelling us to try and find meaning in this event along with her. As in the labyrinth image above, circu-larity takes us to our own heart as well as the story's heart.

Third, in keeping with the book's title, the remembering narrator's circling back encapsulates the *year* of magical thinking. The structure reinforces the uniqueness of this span of time. The narrator and her mode of telling keep underscoring that this time is unlike any other.

While Didion could have chosen any number of ways to tell this story, a circular structure forces her to keep digging deeper, burrowing into the emotional center of her loss. Once we've read the story this way, we find it hard to imagine this story told any other way—a key sign that the structure is organic, that it is *right*. Didion's circular structure metaphorically represents her own circling efforts to come to grips with John's death during the year the book covers, because the best structures work on more than one level.

The circular structure interweaves the two yous more often than a chronological structure, which often begins with the remembering self but then continues with only the experiencing one, so a circular structure demands a solid command of both your material and your intentions for your memoir. Even a writer as skilled as Joan Didion required the narrative distance of a number of years before she could successfully navigate these waters. One can easily imagine her sitting at her desk, her various forays into comprehending the incomprehensible spread out around her. It is Didion's anchor—the moment when everything changed—that keeps her circular structure from becoming similarly incomprehensible.

A circular structure's anchor does not have to be its catalyst—although it can be. In *A Month of Sundays: Searching for the Spirit and My Sister*, Julie Mars goes to a different church every Sunday, providing a narrative anchor. In *Heaven's Coast*, Mark Doty often goes for walks, which in turn provide catalysts for his associative wanderings. It's important to bear in mind that attempting such a structure requires a command of narrative and associative skills that not many writers possess. Still, if this structure appeals to you, it can be well worth the effort.

SPOTLIGHT EXERCISE

Reading and writing: The best circularly structured memoirs work because they have a narrative anchor—a touchstone that the remembering narrator (and by association the reader) returns to throughout the story. For such a grounding incident or image to work, it must be powerful enough to support a circular narrative, have larger metaphoric resonance, and have the associative strength to engage your reader. Consider the catalyst you noted at the beginning of this chapter. Is there a touchstone within it? It may not be obvious at first look. Touchstones can be anything from a spot on a wall to the sound of thunder. List some possible touchstones for your own memoir, and if one provides some immediate resonance for you, keep going and see where it takes you. See if you can successfully circle back to it and if it retains its sensuous aura when you do.

Associative Structure

Mark Doty's *Heaven's Coast*, whose catalyst—the death of a beloved partner—
is similar to Didion's, employs a different structure. Doty's plot proceeds
through scenes that move backward and forward from the moment his partner, Wally, is diagnosed with AIDS. Doty, a poet, often connects these moments
through strong images, with one image or sequence leading the writer to
another. Doty's memoir is told through *association*, where one event or memory stimulates another.

In an *associative structure*, the scenes are linked by a quality,
a mood, a connection. This structure feels "natural," as memory
itself arises from such cues or triggers.

Chapter titles in this memoir also evoke this structure: for example, "A Shore
Walk" is followed by "House Finches" and then "Dancing." The chapter titled
"Refuge" begins with "We bought a cabin in the woods—a camp, in Vermont
parlance" (162). The next chapter, "Refuge (2)," starts with "Provincetown,
1990" (173). The details of living in one place lead the writer (and reader)
associatively to another place. An advantage of an associative structure is the
strong emotional connection writer and reader share when moving from one
part of the narrative to another. Chronology isn't the point; the sense of story
is. As memory itself is associative, it's not surprising that many memoirs are
told this way. For example, a person at a funeral immediately thinks of the last
time he or she lost a loved one.

In contrast to Didion's experience, in this instance the death occurs not
suddenly but over a period of years, allowing the writer to document the pro-
gression of Wally's illness and how it changes both Mark's and Wally's lives.
The occasion of the death and the lead-up to it spark memories of specific
houses as well as the places and friends that marked their life together.

Doty's command of associative reflection results in a powerful meditation
on mortality and how it illuminates life along with the specific details surrounding the narrator and his partner as they face this challenge. *Heaven's
Coast*'s metaphysical dimensions emerge strongly and poetically within this
imagistic structure. The memories and events acquire momentum through
this associational accretion of detail.

We call the deepening of meaning through juxtaposing events and images
that reinforce each other *scaffolding*. Just as a building is much more than the

sum of its rooms, a story's total impact exceeds the effect of any single event or image. Your structure benefits from scaffolding in several ways. One is that the meaning becomes implicit as well as explicit as the writer—and the reader—create resonance by juxtaposing various telling details, narrative lines of action, and images. Another is the connection created with readers through association: even though it is the author's story, readers make it their own via identification with the imagery and emotion the author shares. The associative structure allows the reader to experience and, in a way, *build* the narrative with the experiencing narrator. It's a powerful tool.

Scaffolding refers to the metaphoric connections of disparate events in a story to create a larger, more resonant meaning.

Doty's choice of structure allows him to create a sense of his and Wally's life together over time. Underpinning the story are the things that ground us: walks (as noted earlier), nature, places the two lived together, people they knew. Through these and other associative links, the reader comes to feel the length and quality of a long relationship and its particularity.

Association is a common memoir structure; it seems natural, as in life some things, people, and events do remind us of others and become the fabric of memory. There is always a danger that the reader may occasionally be lost: When did that happen? How did that event trigger something else? However, texture and quality, a sense of felt life, are the rewards in such a structure, and Doty's memoir is rich, rewarding reading.

SPOTLIGHT EXERCISE

Writing: Associating memories with a place or a time period allows us to begin to develop a sense of interlocking events, in turn leading us to plot. Draw a time line on a piece of paper and begin to insert key places and occurrences. Do some notations connect to others or associate with other times in your life? Alternatively, if you're a spatial person, set up physical markers in a room that represent key events. As you move from one marker to another, see if you can come up with a gesture that expresses it. Do you walk more quickly or slowly to certain events? That body response helps you create rhythm in your narrative and gives you clues about where you'd like to augment the details.

Collage Structure

A structure related to the associative structure is one we'll call *collage*, where episodes (usually very short ones) are "pasted up" against other episodes. An example is Abigail Thomas's memoir *Safekeeping*, in which vignettes from her life in the 1960s on are presented in very short chapters. Many chapters are less than one page, as in, for example, "My Name," which is just three sentences long: "You had a certain way of saying my name. It was the inflection maybe, something you put in those three syllables. And now you are gone and my name is just my name again, not the story of my life" (165).

A *collage* structure juxtaposes discrete events against one another; the reader fills in the gaps, making meaning by forging connections between events that seem unrelated.

Thomas's snapshots have titles like "To Keep Him Company," "Insomnia," and "Skipping Stones." Several involve conversations with Thomas's sister. The moments of each chapter are distilled and acute. Together they indeed represent a life, as the subtitle of the book indicates: "some true stories from a life." Some of the chapters are first person, some third, and occasionally the reader is knit into the narrator with "you," the address of the second person. The writer's life emerges in much the same way that we make sense of a photograph album—specific images reach out from the neutral background to capture our attention. The result is imagistic, poignant or funny or quizzical, the fragments cohering into a whole.

Reader participation is an advantage of the collage structure—the short episodes leave gaps in the narrative for the reader to fill. As each sequence is satisfying and complete, readers could choose to read the chapters out of sequence, further creating their own narratives. The brevity of the episodes adds to their power, their punch. Readers who prefer to be lost in a continuous narrative may find this approach less satisfying, as the gaps make them aware that they are reading. In other words, the collage structure disrupts their sense of what a "story" is. For readers who like the challenge of cocreating the work, however, the collage structure is enticing.

Some memoirs employ elements of a collage structure in their use of images, lengthy epigraphs, and stories that serve as forewords or preludes to chapters. Such a book is Mira Bartók's *The Memory Palace*. While told associatively, the sections represent parts of the memory palace of the title. For example, a discourse called "The Year of the Horse" is followed by a Bedouin quotation, *"Thou shall fly without wings, and conquer without any sword. Oh, horse . . ."* (141), followed by a chapter heading, "Death, the Rider," and a photograph of what appears to be an ancient frieze. And then the narrative resumes. These juxtapositions, including the illustrations, present a gloss on the text for those who wish to linger. Other readers may glance at these and immerse themselves more fully in the story. Again, the choice is the reader's.

SPOTLIGHT EXERCISE

Writing: Imagine your story as a collection of objects. List the objects, then describe the textures and qualities of these objects in a notebook. Alternatively, think of a key event in your life and try to envision it as a series of photographs. What is the quality of the light in the images? What is the overall mood or tone of the pictures? The sensory details you'll record in this exercise will help you to create strong physical/textural details in your story.

Parallel Structure

While by its very nature the memoir form makes us aware of a writer in the present looking back, some writers accentuate the gaps in time by using a historical plot or someone else who lived in the past as juxtaposition for their own story. This type of structure adds complexity and dramatizes the two yous vividly. A variation of this form in staged solo performance is called *auto/biography*, an intersection between "the autobiographical self of the writer-performer" with "the biographical record of the historical personage" (Miller, Taylor, and Carver, *Voices Made Flesh*, 7).

A *parallel structure* contrasts two time periods and often two people, creating deeper meaning via a rich, parallel narrative.

In a parallel structure, the historical story juxtaposes another's journey against the present narrator's in an effort to create a parallel plot that enhances both lives. Such a memoir is *Back Talk: Teaching Lost Selves to Speak* by Joan Weimer, which tells the story of Weimer's debilitating back surgery and recovery against that of the nineteenth-century American writer (and grandniece of James Fenimore Cooper) Constance Fenimore Woolson, who lived part of her life abroad. Mystery surrounded Woolson's life, particularly her relationship with Henry James. Her death after she fell from a window in Venice prompted speculation about whether the fall was accidental or suicide.

Weimer's back injury forces her to change and rediscover the parts of her self that have been overshadowed by her successful academic career: "Probably I'd had good reasons for shoving them into a cage and hiding it in a dark corner. But now I'd need to release those ghostly selves, to brush aside the cobwebs and open that cage. To my astonishment, I'd find the key to its rusted lock in the hands of Constance Fenimore Woolson" (9).

Speculating about Woolson's motives for her writing, her travels, and her relationship with James allows Weimer to uncover buried stories of her own past. Julie Powell accomplishes a similar excavation in her best-selling memoir, *Julie and Julia: 365 Days, 524 Recipes, 1 Tiny Apartment Kitchen*, her journey to becoming an accomplished cook through the recipes, and life, of Julia Child.

This structure bestows a double consequence on the story, as two lives are intertwined. The past gives the present ballast as well, underscoring parallels that provide insight into the writer's own story. Readers often appreciate the historical detail, enjoying the opportunity to see their present world through the prism of the past.

Perhaps the greatest challenges of the parallel structure are, first, transforming research about the past into dramatic scenes and, second, the danger

---

SPOTLIGHT EXERCISE

Reading and writing: Joan Weimer was already researching the life of Constance Fenimore Woolson when her back problems began, but using Woolson's life as a vehicle for mirroring Weimer's own difficulties occurred to her only over time. Nonetheless, we are drawn to certain historical characters because something about their lives resonates for us. The two of us, for example, return again and again to the life and work of Katherine Anne Porter, a writer born in challenging circumstances who transformed herself into a woman of letters, as we make sense of our own lives as writers.

Are there people from the past whose lives fascinate you? They don't necessarily need to be public figures—our own ancestors can provide keys to current dilemmas in our own lives. Take a moment to make a list of historical people by whom you're intrigued. If one seems to provide particular resonance, make a note of that, too, and, if you wish, write a few paragraphs to see where that person takes you.

that the reader might get more immersed in the historical life than the present one. The historic details may appear richer or more intriguing because they are less familiar, less pedestrian than our own lives seem to be when we're living them, and writers can often imagine the lives of others more dramatically than they can their own. The writer who uses a parallel structure must balance the two stories, making sure that the historical plot provides a gloss on the life of the memoir writer and promotes understanding of his or her story.

Weimer's memoir does not "solve" the mysteries surrounding Woolson's life. Rather, it draws wisdom from a woman's struggle to be an artist in an earlier time, underscoring the particularities of Weimer's own personal journey as well as its gifts and conflicts.

Locational Structure

By now it's clear that there are many possibilities for structuring your memoir. Our selections are not exhaustive, as, really, only the imagination limits the containers we can use for our stories. We'll consider one last one here, that of the locational structure, which uses landscape or setting as grounding for the interior passage. Elizabeth Gilbert organizes her best-selling memoir *Eat, Pray, Love* in this way; as her subtitle states, her work is "one woman's search for everything across Italy, India and Indonesia."

A *locational structure* uses place or setting to ground the various segments of the narrative.

While Gilbert's memoir takes the reader on a far and free-ranging quest for love and experience in foreign lands, another memoir using this structure, Julie Mars's *A Month of Sundays*, is subtitled *Searching for the Spirit and My Sister* and takes a different tack. After caring for her sister, Shirley, who dies of pancreatic cancer, for seven months, Mars goes in search of spiritual meaning. Her book takes place over thirty-one weeks, during which she goes to a different church or spiritual center in Albuquerque, New Mexico, or upstate New York every Sunday. Mars describes her task and her method in her preface: "I will go to church every Sunday for thirty-one weeks, a month of Sundays. I will dress up and arrive a half hour early to take a picture with Shirley's simple camera. . . . I will enter the church five minutes early and sit somewhere in the middle. I will open myself to the spirit" (xvi).

Mars's structure allows her to proceed in a manner similar to either the associative structure or the collage structure we discussed earlier. Mars, however, uses each location as a stepping-off point for reminiscences of her past, of Shirley's illness and funeral, of Mars's own spiritual awakening. Often during a chapter one or more days are highlighted with a subhead like "Friday" or "Thursday." Mars uses these weekday events before she visits a specific church as associative springboards.

Landscape has always been a powerful motivator for memoir—consider Gretel Erlich's *The Solace of Open Spaces* and Edward Abbey's *Desert Solitaire*, to name but two. We organize our lives around the places we've lived or in which we wish we'd lived, around moves in childhood or adulthood, around places we've visited, or around rooms in other people's houses. Our bodies in space provide much of our sensory stimulation and mark the crucial passages we've negotiated. It makes sense that such sensory moments might provide the catalysts from which we begin our memoir.

The strength of a locational structure is that it's immediately evocative, as details of place underpin experience or overlie comprehension. Because our brains locate or isolate details to make sense of what's happening to us, this structure is particularly powerful for a reader. It demands sensory detail in setting scene, an essential skill that we'll detail further in chapter 5. The sudden shifts in locations can interrupt a narrative, but for a skilled memoirist, this too can add to the pleasure readers find as they unravel the weaving of the story's separate strands.

SPOTLIGHT EXERCISE

Reading and writing: Often, when we say "place," we think of larger places—houses, cities, office buildings, and the like. But "place" encompasses smaller places, too—your childhood room, for example, or the restaurant where you meet friends each week.

Do the places in your life organize themselves into some cohesive theme, like Mars's places of worship or Gilbert's three countries that begin with the letter *I*? Are there commonalities among the places you've lived, the rooms where you've spent a lot of time, or are there patterns to your movement to or away from them? Make a list of places, large or small, that have figured in your life. Then draw some lines between them, not limiting yourself to obvious, immediate connections like chronology but instead thinking associatively. Write the association that precipitated the connection on the line itself. (Use a different color, if you like.) Play with these places, trying to imagine a memoir that uses them as its structure.

CHOOSING A STRUCTURE

One of the most frequent concerns we hear from those contemplating writing a memoir is that the story the author wants to tell is overwhelming. Considering structure not only addresses this dilemma but also helps you move past it.

The best structure for your story is one that allows your narrative to flow organically, providing a flexibility that will allow your story to breathe while at the same time establishing constraints that sufficiently focus it. The central issues of your story, including the main conflicts, determine its structure.

You and Your Audience

In this early stage of imagining the shape of your story, we find that it's helpful to think about the impact on the reader you'd ideally like your memoir to have. Consider these questions carefully:

- Do you want your audience foremost to learn about the qualities of a place, a person, or a time?
- Do you want to persuade the reader of a particular point of view or moral position about your subject?
- Do you want, like many first-person narrators of fiction, to explore the motivations and the causality of actions taken during a critical period of your life?

There is no correct answer to the state of mind or feeling you'd like the reader to experience, but a clear sense of what you'd like to achieve will aid you in making narrative decisions. As we've often told our students, no one story can accomplish everything. Some key chapters in our lives are so complex that to really represent them would require several books. Your job is to zero in on your intentions for this one project via your desire to take your reader on this particular journey with you.

We believe that one of the reasons we write memoirs is to explore who we were at the stage in our lives we are writing about. One of the paradoxes of writing a memoir is that through the act of burrowing deeply into the past, we come to better understand where we are now and how we got there. In a sense, writing a memoir is an act of identity construction and reconstruction.

Writing the memoir is one way of learning what was previously unknowable about ourselves while at the same time giving ourselves the luxury of exploring this in the company of a witness, the reader. As Vivian Gornick notes, "When Rousseau observes, 'I have nothing but myself to write about, and this self that I have, I hardly know of what it consists,' he is saying to the reader, 'I will go in search of it in your presence . . . and together we'll see what it exemplifies'" (92).

SPOTLIGHT EXERCISE

Writing: A good place to begin your consideration of what structure might work for you is with an informal list of what you hope your audience will take away from your memoir. Mention ideas as well as feelings. For example, do you hope that a story about a dear friend's illness will prompt the reader to discover the gifts as well as the tolls of the illness? This list will point you not only toward events you'll want to include but also, more importantly, toward the aspects of the self you wish to reveal in this project.

Creating the World of Your Story

Your list of what you want to explore with your audience and what you hope they will take away with them through reading your memoir will help you clarify your motives in writing. These motives naturally lead to conflicts or blockages—the things that arrested you or stood in your way, as we discussed early in the chapter. It is the nature of these conflicts that leads to structural decisions.

As we mentioned in chapter 1, people read memoirs to immerse themselves in the details of another person's life. Thus we read Eudora Welty's *One Writer's Beginnings* or Oscar Hijuelos's *Thoughts without Cigarettes* to experience the individual paths each of these writers followed to become artists. We expect the course of these lives to be unpredictable and messy and hopefully touched with grace, just as our own lives are. But we continue to read in order to inhabit the world of another, in all its richness and startling detail. World creation brings us back to structure and how we can create a shape for the world we wish to share.

For many writers, capturing a sense of the time and place in which they grew up drives their desire to create a memoir. Sharman Apt Russell's *Standing in the Light: My Life as a Pantheist*, for example, is so grounded in southwestern New Mexico that she includes a map at the beginning of the book. Her occasion of the telling highlights the importance of geography: "My title . . . comes from the Quaker phrase 'to stand in the Light,' a concept with many meanings, encompassing political beliefs as well as spiritual. In my case, it is very much related to the bright New Mexico sky. . . . [P]antheism is a word whose back I ride like a man on a horse trying to get somewhere. Or maybe a word more like a house, a place of shelter when it is cold and rainy, a house with big windows and a gorgeous view" (xiv).

As we mentioned in chapter 2, Annie Dillard's *An American Childhood*, grounded in Pittsburgh and western Pennsylvania, also excels at world creation. Dillard accomplishes a stunning weave of the internal life of her young self growing up in the 1950s with the physical manifestations of trees, rivers, and the topography of her neighborhood. She is a master at creating the *emblematic moment* that stands for an emotional realization as well. When she describes, for example, the simple joy of childhood, of racing full tilt down a city street for the pure pleasure of it, she gives us details so that we experience it, too. We see her running and flapping her arms down the sidewalk, feel the pulse of blood in our arms. When at last a fellow pedestrian acknowledges her animal spirits and smiles, Dillard captures the image of their meeting simply but eloquently: "So we passed on the sidewalk—a beautifully upright woman walking in her tan linen suit, a kid running and flapping her arms—we passed on the sidewalk with a look of accomplices who share a humor just beyond irony. What's a heart for?" (109).

The *emblematic moment* is an image or complex of images metaphorical of a larger truth in the story.

FURTHER SPOTLIGHT EXERCISES

Reading: Which of the structures presented in this chapter allow you, given your subject matter and/or the occasion of the telling, the most possibilities for discovery?

Writing: Choose one structure and sketch out what it might allow you to reveal. Are there disadvantages to this structure that you can see? Is it restrictive in any way? How?

Reading and writing: Write down the qualities you enjoy most in a narrative. Choose one of the memoirs discussed in this chapter that has some of those qualities. How does its structure contribute to your reading enjoyment?

As you review the examples of structures covered above, the degree of reader participation as well as the imperatives of the occasion of the telling will lead you to consider a particular one—associative, perhaps, or circular, for example, if your goal is to meditate upon a time. Along the way, you'll open yourself to a deeper understanding of the you that you were then and how it shaped the you that you have become.

The kind of world you want to create and share with your reader leads you to the container that best holds your story. In chapter 4 we'll delve into the workings of scene and how to transform particular events into detailed, dramatic, and vivid moments in your memoir.

4

Arranging the Scenes

Giving Them Muscle

> What the aspiring memoirist *can* learn ... is the use of emblematic scenes—where one spotlit moment has the effect of standing in for, or symbolizing, a whole larger situation.
>
> —SVEN BIRKERTS, *The Art of Time in Memoir: Then, Again*

Plot controls the arc of events, including its rising and falling action. Plot's building blocks are *scenes*, doorways into your story that allow readers to experience not only moments from your life but also your point of view. Just as you use structure and plot to build a form for your story, well-written scenes are mirrors that readers can pass through to forget their own lives as they immerse themselves in your story's world.

Scenes are moments in motion whose developing action (internal or external) engages and keeps the reader's interest.

But what, precisely, is a scene, and how do you build one? To begin to answer that question, let's consider a relatively short scene from Penelope Lively's memoir *Oleander, Jacaranda: A Childhood Perceived*.

We are going by car from Bulaq Dakhur to Heliopolis. I am in the back. The leather of the seat sticks to my bare legs. We travel along a road lined at either side with oleander and jacaranda trees, alternate splashes of white and blue. I chant, quietly: "Jacaranda, oleander ... Jacaranda, oleander ..." And as I do so there comes to me the revelation that in a few hours' time we shall return by the same route and that I shall pass the same trees, in reverse order—oleander, jacaranda, oleander, jacaranda—and that, by the same token, I can look back upon myself now, of this moment. I shall be able to think about myself now, thinking this—but it will be then, not now. (1)

We've chosen this scene to begin our discussion of dramatic structure because in a brief space it contains all the elements of scene we'll be covering in this chapter: the particularizing of a moment, immediacy (in this case, through the use of present tense), powerful language that helps conjure the scene for the reader, telling details that create a picture in the reader's mind, and dialogue that invites the reader into the scene, along with an emblematic moment that both stands for and enhances the larger narrative. As you'll see, a strong scene involves the reader's senses and engages the reader's mind and emotions.

This scene begins at a specific moment ("We are going in the car . . ."), with a telling detail ("The leather of the seat sticks to my bare legs") and action (in this case, internal action, which we'll discuss at the end of this chapter) that rises from that moment to an *epiphany* ("I shall be able to think about myself now, thinking this") that provides closure to the scene while at the same time generating a connection between the writer and the reader.

> An *epiphany* is a moment of realization or heightened
> awareness that can lead to change in the protagonist.

Documenting a compact scene that really happened and at the same time contains all of these elements can seem a daunting prospect. And yet, everything you need to construct such a moment resides either in your memory or in your imagination and can be accessed via the Fiction Writer's Toolkit. What's important to bear in mind is what Annie Dillard reminds us in "To Fashion a Text": "Don't hope . . . to preserve your memories. If you prize your memories as they are, by all means avoid . . . writing a memoir. . . . The Work battens on your memories. And it replaces them" (70).

The dance between memory and creating scenes that come to life—the movement, that is, between the two yous—is the heart of a memoir that resonates with readers: they experience events that match your narrator's memories. As we discussed in chapter 1, what you're after is the essential truth of your story, even more than exactly "what happened," which is nearly always impossible to reconstruct. In this chapter, we'll show you how dramatic structure can help you mold scenes that come to vivid life.

As we discuss dramatic structure, keep in mind that each of these steps applies to your larger work as well. When an artist creates a large painting, she considers each section's particular shapes and relationships. Like an artist, visualize your work as a canvas, with scenes making up chapters and chapters mimicking the larger plot. Scenes and chapters, in other words, are microcosms of the arc of the completed story.

DRAMATIC STRUCTURE

The single most important thing you can do when crafting a memoir is to keep your reader's attention. Dramatic structure is your means to this end. A scene's structure begins with an immediate entrance into what's happening on the page by providing a protagonist with whom the reader wishes to spend time and an image that immerses the reader at once into a moment from that narrator's life. Scene structure sets what Lisa Dale Norton calls "shimmering images" into motion.

Dramatic structure organizes both scenes and the larger work into a coherent whole that moves forward from its opening moment.

Consider Penelope Lively's scene above. The protagonist is a child, someone who notices things like the sticky leather seat and the passing trees, and at the same time an adult who possesses the author's resources of language and experience. Toggling between the child's sense of the moment and her own adult capacity for transforming memory into language, Lively provides an immediate entrance into the scene and immerses the reader in the moment. To the reader, this action appears effortless. For you the writer, it's a skill you'll master through study and practice.

The tools of scene structure allow you, the writer, to share the experience of you, the subject, with readers via telling details and emblematic moments. Scenes—the building blocks of dramatic structure—particularize the general, offering moving pictures of time in motion, each with a beginning, a middle, and an end, as Lively does in the scene above.

ORDERING THE SCENE

No matter where it begins or ends, no matter how long it takes, no matter what happens over its course, every scene—and your larger work, because every scene is a miniplot—should contain each of the following steps in this order:

catalyst → conflict → rising action → climax → denouement

The *catalyst* is the moment in time at which a scene begins to
move. The *conflict* involves the oppositions, internal or external,
facing the protagonist. The *rising action* deepens the oppositions
the protagonist faces. The *climax* is a scene's epiphanic
moment—the turn, the shift, the pivot point. The scene's
denouement provides closure.

Before we show you each of these steps in more detail, here's a brief illustration from a film with which you're likely familiar. After the war is over in *Gone with the Wind*, Scarlett O'Hara realizes that she won't be able to hang on to Tara unless she has some money (catalyst). Deciding that the best possible source of money will be Rhett Butler but at the same time certain that he mustn't see how destitute she's become (conflict), Scarlett storms from room to room in her patched dress, searching the few things left for something to help her out of her dilemma (rising action). Then she spots her mother's green velvet curtains, gets that familiar twinkle in her eye, and begins to yank them down (climax). This scene's denouement actually begins the next scene, as we see Scarlett strutting along a city boardwalk in a lovely green velvet dress.

Catalyst, conflict, rising action, climax, denouement: these are the tools you can use to create living, lively scenes. We call the movement among these elements the *story arc*. Successful story arcs plant expectations in the reader and then satisfy them, creating one of the core pleasures of narrative.

Story arc refers to the movement among the elements of
dramatic structure that form a narrative.

Catalyst

Just as the occasion of the telling, which we discussed in depth in chapter 1, launches the beginning of a memoir, every scene begins with a defining moment, a catalyst that instigates everything that comes after. The scene that opens this chapter, for example, begins with the young Penelope Lively sitting on that hot, sticky leather seat in the back of the car. The scene above is ignited by Scarlett's need for money to save Tara.

As evidenced by these examples, a scene's catalyst does not need (or even want) to be particularly dramatic in and of itself. In fact, many scenes—the strongest scenes—begin in the mundane and regular. As we noted in a different context in chapter 2, in *The Year of Magical Thinking*, Joan Didion returns again and again to just such a scene—the moment before dinner when her husband, John, asks for another glass of Scotch, a snapshot in time that then suddenly escalates into (and beyond) the moment he dies.

What's key to building a scene is that within each moment is *desire*. Who wants what? Even in Didion's routine moment just before John dies there is desire, her desire for everything to remain the same: his desire for a second glass of Scotch and her desire for him not to die. Notice that in this case these desires can't be articulated in that prior moment. It is often the case, in memoir (and in life), that we "don't know what [we] got (till it's gone)."

SPOTLIGHT EXERCISE

Writing: Think for a moment of the spotlit moments you recorded in chapter 1. The fact that these memories remain with you suggests that they are catalysts, fragments from which individual scenes might unspool. Even if you can't recall what happened after the key image, writing it down will often unstop the memories you think you've lost.

So, without thinking about it, pick one of those moments now. Consider what has brought you, its protagonist, to this moment. Is there someone else in the picture? Who wants what? Make some notes as answers come to you. By the end of this chapter you'll have used this spotlit moment to create a complete scene. Working on one scene at a time can keep you from being overwhelmed by the idea of writing your whole story.

At the same time, be aware, as Patricia Hampl points out in *I Could Tell You Stories*, that your initial creation of this scene may contain some elements that don't belong there. This isn't a problem; always bear in mind that your first attempt at recording a spotlit moment is a draft—a starting point for digging deeper. As soon as we begin to write about the past our memories toss in all sorts of subliminal detritus. One of the great joys of writing memoir is that we'll get to sort this detritus into a larger truth, discarding what isn't essential and expanding upon what is. It's important at this generative stage not to censor or edit but simply to let the story emerge.

Desire is the great motivator, driving practically every moment of our lives, and motivation forces us to act and make choices. Even something as basic as being hungry involves desire, and memoir can be driven by such basic needs as well as more complex ones.

Conflict

Conflict stands at cross-purposes to desire and thus drives scene. That's why we asked you above, Who wants what? Where desire is a catalyst, conflict is created when someone or something stands in your—or your character's—way. So, even while Joan Didion wishes for everything to remain the same, John's sudden death changes everything.

While the word itself conjures slings and arrows, conflict does not necessarily require the tools of battle to be compelling to the reader. Conflict can be internal or external, as we'll discuss later in this chapter. At its simplest, internal conflict involves a battle with oneself. As a human being you know that drill all too well. As a writer you can mine that internal struggle to create compelling scenes. Didion's conflict in *The Year of Magical Thinking* is both internal and external—her internal desire for continuity upended by an external reality, John's sudden death.

SPOTLIGHT EXERCISE

Writing: Consider the spotlit moment you noted above. There you are at an earlier moment in your life, captured in a still photograph in your mind's eye. Now, using what you wanted in that moment, put that photograph in motion. You want ——. But —— stands in your way.

Maybe you're sitting on a swing and want to keep swinging higher and higher, but it's getting dark, and you have to be home before dark. Conflict.

Maybe you've been forbidden to see the person who has just called you, but you want to see them. Conflict.

Maybe you're scowling at someone outside the frame. Why? Conflict.

Maybe there's a war on, and you must get out of the place you are in. Conflict.

Record any sensory images of that conflict: qualities of light, expression, gesture.

Nearly every moment of our lives exists in counterpoint to something or someone standing in its way. Consider, for example, the beginning of Tobias Wolff's memoir *This Boy's Life*, which we cited in chapter 3. While young Toby and his mother may desire stability, their peripatetic life stands in sharp contrast to this desire. Conflict is the gunpowder of dramatic structure, propelling the catalyst.

Rising Action

The moment a catalyst is fired by conflict, the action begins to rise. We like to think of rising action as a deepening of oppositions, as the protagonist and the situation move farther and farther into the conflict.

This is an excellent moment to bring up the issue of time. We humans tend to think in chronological terms—this happened, then that happened. But when it comes to rising action, moments from the past or the future can deepen the opposition in surprising ways. Using such moments in your narrative can up the ante for both your narrator and your dramatic structure. Linearity is not necessary in rising action; psychological conflict often proceeds in a montage of moments. Such juxtaposition can enhance the conflict.

We use the term *chronos* (the Greek word for "time," as in "chronology") to refer to clock time, while *kairos* (the Greek term for "holy" or "sacred time") defines the sense of time in which a moment can expand and seem like hours or contract and feel as if no time has passed at all. Think about crucial instances in your life during which time seemed to expand or contract along with your sensory apprehension of what was happening. Intriguingly, especially for our purposes in writing memoir, memory distorts (or enhances) our sense of kairos even further.

While we may recall time sequentially, within our minds all our moments— past, present, and future—exist in a present all their own. Even as you're reading this sentence (present), you may be thinking about what you had for lunch (past) or what you'll have for dinner (future). Applying this capacity of the mind to a scene's rising action can increase the tension, as Sven Birkerts notes: "Not only is the sequential approach a chore for the writer, but it's often a deadly bore for the reader. The point is *story*, not chronology, and in memoir the story all but requires *the dramatic ordering that hindsight affords*. The question is not what happened when, but what, for the writer, was the path of realization" (61, emphasis added). This is yet another instance where the remembering you has a distinct advantage—all that time before and since has affected both the scene and your memory of it.

Joan Didion uses chronos and kairos to marvelous effect in *The Year of Magical Thinking*, returning again and again to the moment before John's death and then examining it from myriad angles with the urgent hope of changing it. In a scene halfway through the book, for example, Didion has just reread one of John's books, *Harp*, in which he imagines a character's death ("'a moment of terror as he realized the inevitable outcome of the accident, then an instant later the eternal dark?'" [155]). Didion wonders if John experienced his own death that way. She then thinks through the seemingly random event that is a heart attack, "a sudden spasm" as plaque clogs the artery, and, deprived of blood and oxygen, the heart starves. "But how did he experience it? The 'moment of terror,' the 'eternal dark'?" she wonders (156).

We use this example for rising action intentionally. The catalyst—Didion's rereading of John's book—is fired by her continued attempts throughout the book to come to terms with his death. Thus the conflict in this scene arises from Didion's application (present) of John's own words (past) to his death (a different moment in the past). But, this being Didion, she then deepens the opposition by pulling back, pulling herself out of the narrative and instead using more abstract language to describe what happens during a heart attack, causing the action to rise and the reader to become more deeply invested in the scene.

The effect of this contemplation is a stunning example of one of the most important lessons we are taught when we begin studying writing. "Be specific," we are told (and teach): the more specific the language, the more individual the moment, and the more universal the connection. While to the layperson Didion's use of less accessible medical terminology in her quiet recitation of facts may seem at first a more difficult approach, in the end Didion achieves a far deeper connection with the reader, rendering the terror of an individual heart attack all the more horrific through the specificity of the language. Didion then brings it home in the two sentences that follow, the first in a paragraph of its own: "But how did he experience it? The 'moment of terror,' the 'eternal dark'?" These two sentences of conjecture exist *outside of time*— or put another way, in kairos time, rather than in chronos, chronological time.

SPOTLIGHT EXERCISE

Reading: Consider the catalyst you recorded earlier in this chapter. What did the you in that moment want, and what stood in your way? What happens when you put that moment into motion? Does dialogue spring forth, an exchange where you express your desire and someone else says no? Or are you sitting in your childhood room, *imagining* what might happen if you attempt to fulfill your desire? Or does this scene occur *after* your desire was thwarted? In the latter two instances, your scene will immediately move into a moment outside the story's chronological time frame to deepen the opposition—in the first case into an imagined future, in the latter into the past. We'll consider the use of flashbacks, and "flashforwards," in chapter 5.

Rising action is integral to the movement of a scene, ratcheting up the tension and therefore the consequences. If at any moment a reader's attention lags, the action is no longer rising. Especially in memoir, the "but it really happened" issue comes into play. When we write memoir, we *shape* what really happened into scenes with deepening oppositions, scenes that *move* toward something the reader cannot yet discern but desires to discover because of the way we've built the scenes. To paraphrase T. S. Eliot, desire is movement. We don't alter the truth; we render it vivid in order to engage the reader and to describe as fully as we can the essence of our experience.

If you think of time in your writing as part of "the mind of your story," emulating how all time exists concurrently in your mind, you can use the manipulation of past, present, and future to move around in time and enhance the rising action of your scenes.

Reversals

While not one of the steps in dramatic structure, *reversals* nonetheless play an important role in maintaining engagement with your reader. Reversals are just what the word implies: a flipping over of what's expected, sending the narrative off in a different direction. A clear reversal occurs in the 2010 remake of *True Grit*, when the heroine vanquishes her antagonist, driving him off a cliff. She feels exultant briefly until the reversal, when she steps back and suddenly falls into a snake pit.

Reversals are unexpected events that send the narrative in a new direction.

In *The Year of Magical Thinking* (and in all her work), Joan Didion refuses to settle for the usual. In this instance, "the usual" might be that when a husband dies, a widow will mourn, and then she will move on. All of this is in fact typically the case, but by adding her refusal to accept the fact of John's death to the mix, Didion can apply everything from attempts to rewrite the past to research into a variety of topics in her effort to change the course of what's already happened. Here, for example, she "reads an explanation, by Vamik D. Volkan, M.D., a professor of psychiatry at the University of Virginia in Charlottesville, of what he called 're-grief therapy,' a technique . . . for the treatment of 'established pathological mourners'" (55). After quoting from Dr. Volkan's findings at some length, Didion reacts thusly:

But where exactly did Dr. Volkan and his team . . . derive their unique under-standing of "the psychodynamics involved in the patient's need to keep the lost one alive," their special ability to "explain and interpret the relationship that had existed between the patient and the one who died"? Were you watching *Tenko* with me and "the lost one" in Brentwood Park, did you go to dinner with us at Morton's? Were you with me and "the one who died" at Punchbowl in Honolulu four months before it happened? Did you gather up plumeria blossoms with us . . . ? (56)

Didion continues this litany of moments with John for another half page before she stops herself and "realize[s] that I am directing irrational anger toward the entirely unknown Dr. Volkan in Charlottesville" (57). Her reali-zation that she is projecting her anger about John's death onto the unknown Dr. Volkan provides a stunning reversal, an acknowledgment that, as Dr. Volkan suggests, she is "'not only upset mentally but . . . unbalanced physi-cally'" (ibid.). Didion's refusal to accept anything given at face value has led her to this moment and is a driving force in the rising action not only of her scenes but also of the entire narrative. In this way she *witnesses* her own

---

SPOTLIGHT EXERCISE

Reading and writing: Not all scenes have reversals, but we've found that when writers employ them, readers are "hooked" all the more. In a sense, the workings of plot and scene weave the reader into the action. Consider the scene you've been working on through the exercises in this chapter. Does something unexpected happen that surprises either the experiencing you or the remembering you? Bear in mind, too, that seemingly unrelated external occurrences can affect a narrator: something as simple as a bluebird's trill might cause someone to realize that life is worth living after all, or a neighbor's dog's incessant barking might drive her in the opposite direction.

The experiencing narrator can effect a reversal as well: the you in the past might be purposefully acting on his desire when he suddenly remembers (and remembering is an internal action) something that causes him to reassess his actions or the behavior of those around him.

Take a few moments here to record a few possible reversals for the scene you're working on. Remember, this is only a draft, a time to explore possibilities. You'll have as much time as you need to revisit it again and again.

experience, one of the great values of writing a memoir. This self-reflexive epiphany derives as well from the interaction of Didion's two yous. In this example, then, the reversal involves a change of mind.

Climax

A scene's climax is its turning point. Yes, in a good scene there have already been reversals that cause rising action to fall until it rises again toward the next crisis. But the climax is the high point, the explosion—whether internal or external—upon which the entire scene pivots.

SPOTLIGHT EXERCISE

Reading and writing: The scene you've been working on in this chapter has been moving toward its own turning point. The drama in a scene's epiphany does not have to be concussive. In fact, the quietest shifts can have far more emotional impact than the loudest explosions. People lean in closer to hear whispers, and readers who must imagine themselves into a scene are more intimately connected to it than those who have been forced in.

This is not to say that your scene won't have a literal explosion at its climax. But as the one who first experienced it and who now is reenvisioning it, you are the one who knows—and records—when the desire and opposition set in motion by your catalyst crescendo to their breaking point.

One of the beauties of the two yous is that there is more than one possible epiphany to your scene. You might apply knowledge you've gained only years after the fact (a letter you don't know about until someone else's death, for example). Even if an external event sends the scene in its moment in a new direction (that trilling bluebird, say), that event might send the experiencing you back to the first time you experienced it and how it made you feel. Recall the young Annie Dillard we referenced in chapter 3, recording her child-self acknowledged by the passing woman who notes Annie's exuberance.

Rather than demand only one climax for your scene during this first draft, we suggest that you instead list as many possibilities as you can, considering how the scene's present, past, and future might affect it. Don't worry about structure, spelling, or grammar—don't even try for complete sentences at this point unless they come naturally. Just note as many possible climaxes as you can.

As noted above, *The Year of Magical Thinking* uses primarily internal action and nonlinear structure to interweave its scenes. Such a structure can reach a climactic point just as dramatically (if not more so) as a linear one. In the scene that follows, Didion begins, "Grief turns out be a place none of us know until we reach it" (188). She then continues her musing, noting that, while we all know we will at some point lose someone close to us, we cannot imagine much beyond our initial shock: "We do not expect this shock to be obliterative, dislocating to both body and mind" (ibid.).

Notice how Didion builds from her catalyst here. Using repetitive structure and opposition, the catalyst of her first sentence ("Grief turns out be a place none of us know until we reach it") crescendos toward a place she did not anticipate. She suspects that the days after John's death will be the most difficult and that "hypothetical healing" will begin after the funeral pushes her beyond her endurance: "We have no way of knowing that this will not be the issue. We have no way of knowing that the funeral itself will be anodyne, a kind of narcotic regression in which we are wrapped in the care of others" (188–89).

In the two sentences above, Didion reverses direction and pushes the scene's tension to its breaking point, its climax. The scene has been built based on what we imagine, what we anticipate. It pivots on what "we have no way of knowing." The tension in this scene occurs because both what we imagine and what we have no way of knowing *exist in the future*—an unknown territory. The unknown, especially concerning the losses each of us will experience during our lives, is perhaps our greatest fear. Fear creates tension all by itself, but it is Didion's insistent charting and traversing of this unknown territory that give *The Year of Magical Thinking* such power and resonance for the reader.

Denouement

After a scene's climax, the writer offers (and the reader requires) at least a sentence acknowledging what has happened—what has changed, shifted, or even stayed the same. Scenes that end before their denouements feel truncated, because readers expect to feel some kind of closure, however inconclusive, before moving on to what's next.

After the climactic shift in the scene above, Didion moves to a future beyond what the narrator has been imagining into the terrible silence of "unending absence." A lesser writer than Didion might have ended at the climactic moment of realization that "the funeral itself is anodyne." But Didion pushes beyond this moment into an uncharted country, from "the heart of the difference between grief as we imagine it and grief as it is" to "the experience of meaninglessness itself" (189).

Despite the territory (grief), Didion makes magic here. She insists on looking at her subject squarely, with her journalistic eye. She provides the reader with both expectation and reality, *as experienced by her*, and so, in her grief, offers an inadvertent guide to grieving, one that does not shy away from the horror or difficulty or impossibility but instead faces it and tries and fails, again and again, to move on.

A scene's denouement leads the protagonist past its climax into the next episode while at the same time leaving enough uncertain that the reader wants to keep reading. In other words, a successful finish to a scene is a balancing act between resolution and uncertainty—a way of offering readers something to hang onto while at the same time urging them toward whatever's next.

SPOTLIGHT EXERCISE

Writing: Your own scene's denouement will arise out of the architecture you've built of rising, falling, and climactic action. Take a moment now to record the moment *after* each of the epiphanies you imagined for your scene in the previous section. The experiencing you might move forward—or step back. The remembering you might comment, imagine, or conjecture. The important thing is to provide the reader with some sense that the narrator acknowledges what has happened in the scene while at the same time his or her larger narrative arc continues to move forward.

Catalyst. Conflict. Rising action. Climax. Denouement. When you revisit your scenes, consider each of these steps carefully, and, as in Didion's memoir, your scenes will not only resonate with readers but offer connections to their own lives as well.

PARTICULARIZING THE MOMENT

Beyond scene structure, writers strive to bring individual moments to life. Doing this with our only tool, words, can sometimes seem an impossible task, and yet, again and again, writers rise to the occasion, particularizing instances so that readers can not only see them but also hear, taste, touch, and even smell them.

Internal Action

In *An American Childhood*, the young Annie Dillard wants to interrupt her parents because she has made what to her is an important discovery. All winter she's been experimenting with a microscope she was given for Christmas. The beginning of this scene is constructed as leisurely narrative, with Dillard being given the microscope, then several paragraphs as she experiments with it, preparing slides of everything from an onion's skin to a section of cork. She even takes scrapings from her own cheek to see the blood and looks at her urine, only to find that the drop has dried into crystals. Dillard shows readers these details, inviting them into the scene. Then she moves into the moment of discovery: "Finally, late that spring, I saw an amoeba. . . . In the basement at my microscope table I spread a scummy drop of Frick Park puddle water on a slide, peeked in, and lo, there was the famous amoeba. He was as blobby and grainy as his picture; I would have known him anywhere" (148).

At this point, Annie runs upstairs to share her discovery with her parents, only to find that they are relaxing and talking over their after-dinner coffee. Her mother informs her that although she's pleased at what her daughter has discovered, she and Annie's father wish to continue what they are doing. Surprisingly, young Annie is not disappointed or angry at this rejection. Instead, Dillard is thrilled by the realization that, by claiming their time, her parents are giving her permission to have her own life as well.

SPOTLIGHT EXERCISE

Writing: Go back now to your scene's catalyst—the shimmering image with which you began. What did you see, hear, smell, taste, and feel when you first reimagined that moment? Take time to list words and sensory details that you can later use to re-create that image for readers. It's unlikely you'll use them all, so don't worry about that at this point. Even if you don't use them, the excavation you do will reveal itself in a more layered narrative, as we mentioned in the discussion of scaffolding in chapter 3. Simply list things like "blue sky," "smell of coffee," "the feel of the old wood banister" that you can later flesh out, as Dillard has.

Throughout this scene, Dillard moves between external and internal action—but her epiphany occurs internally. Notice how Dillard uses details to particularize the scene—the "blobby and grainy" amoeba, for example. Telling details like this immerse readers in the scene so that they experience its rising action and climax as if they were living it along with the narrator.

External Action

A scene's oppositions can increase by either external or internal action. Up until this point, we've been focusing largely on internal action, as it can be more difficult to chart. But well-written external action can be just as, if not more, riveting. In this scene from Tobias Wolff's *This Boy's Life*, Toby, as most American teenaged boys do, has been experimenting with getting drunk. He and his friends are sitting at the edge of a gully when Toby hops up on a branch that extends over the gully to where it turns to cement. His friends holler at him to stop, but Toby knows he can handle it, and to demonstrate, he bounces on the branch and flaps his arms. Then he puts his hands in his pockets and strolls still farther out, until the branch breaks:

> I didn't feel myself land, but I heard the wind leave me in a rush. I was rolling sideways down the hillside with my hands still in my pockets, rolling around and around like a log, faster and faster, picking up speed on the steep cement. The cement ended in a drop where the earth below had washed away. I flew off the edge and went spinning through the air and landed hard and rolled downhill through the ferns, bouncing over rocks and deadfall, the ferns rustling around me, and then I hit something hard and stopped cold.
>
> I was on my back. I could not move, I could not breathe. I was too empty to take the first breath, and my body would not respond to the bulletins I sent. Blackness came up from the bottom of my eyes. I was drowning, and then I drowned. (189–90)

Notice the verbs that Wolff uses in this passage, how they not only help you visualize the scene but also deepen the oppositions: "strolled," "rolling," "flew," and "spinning" (among others) are all strong, active verbs. When you describe external action, the more work your verbs can do, the stronger and more vivid the scene will be to your reader.

SPOTLIGHT EXERCISE

Writing: Even if the scene you've been working with in this chapter is not external, it nonetheless occurs in some physical space that requires external delineation, and even if it's a quiet space, it nonetheless can be described by active verbs. Your childhood bedroom, for example, might "calm" or "frighten." A coffee shop might "clatter" or "chatter." Make a list of strong verbs that *show* the external action of your scene. As always, you'll return to this later, so don't worry about getting things perfect this first time out.

THE EMBLEMATIC SCENE

We opened this chapter citing Sven Birkerts's use of the term *emblematic scene*. Now that you've learned how to build a scene, one step at a time, you're ready to consider how your scenes can do even more heavy lifting.

> *Emblematic scenes* not only highlight a particular moment
> but represent the memoir's larger themes as well, moving the
> action forward while also serving as microcosms and
> metaphors for the larger work.

Let's return again to the scene with which we opened this chapter and which begins Penelope Lively's memoir *Oleander, Jacaranda*. In this scene the young Penelope is riding in the back of a car with sticky leather seats, reciting the names of the trees, over and over, when she has a sudden insight into the nature of time, apprehending not only that the order of the trees will reverse when she makes the return trip later that day but also that *in future*

SPOTLIGHT EXERCISE

Writing: The examples we've provided of emblematic moments are complex ones, but such moments can be deceptively simple as well. We've noticed that what we call "first-date" stories—the details about ourselves we choose to share when we first meet someone—often contain such moments.

What are your first-date stories? Perhaps you always tell about the time you ran out of gas in the middle of nowhere, or, conversely, how you were the one who figured out how to get a stalled elevator full of people in motion again. Each of these stories reveals something you believe to be emblematic about you—whether or not they truly are. So begin this exercise by writing down your go-to first-date story. Try to write it as you tell it, keeping its dramatic structure to the form you've mastered over the years.

In *The Situation and the Story*, Vivian Gornick notes that memoir requires that the narrator have a stance that sustains his or her story. Once you've recorded your first-date story, put it away for a day or two. Then reread it with an eye toward the stance that you, its narrator, have taken regarding the you in the story. Do you use this story to illustrate what a contrary person you once were? Or to show that you've always been a take-charge sort?

Emblematic moments are keys into the two yous. Pay attention to them, and they'll help you map potential paths for your story.

years she will be able to return to this moment at will, looking at it for further meaning.

Throughout this memoir, Lively uses her memories of growing up in Egypt before and during the early years of World War II as stepping-off points for considering the writer she has become. Using the first moment in which she grasps chronos and kairos and their potential to enable her to reimagine her life, she spotlights how important they will be to her, to the way she writes, and to her search for meaning through her fiction.

PUTTING IT ALL TOGETHER

In this chapter we've broken scene down to its essential components of catalyst, conflict, rising action, climax, and denouement. We've found that it helps some writers to think architecturally about the way scenes work to build the larger plot. The foundation is the occasion of the telling, and each scene takes the reader deeper into the narrative as the writer constructs the building's frame. The building's levels are made up of chapters, each of which is built, scene by scene.

FURTHER SPOTLIGHT EXERCISES

Reading: Pick a scene from a memoir and explore why it does or doesn't work as a scene. Observe the balance of internal and external action. How does the scene engage the reader?

Writing: Create a dynamic scene in your memoir from anywhere in the story. By dynamic we mean a scene that has a dramatic arc, uses sensory details and a specific moment in time/space to reveal character or further the action, or creates a parallel image/event to reinforce a main theme or throughline. Be as specific as you can to *show* the action.

We've talked about how action moves in a scene, but bear in mind that rhythm, the momentum and movement of language and how they "pace" the action, is also important to rising action. Not all scenes or chapters are the same length, for example. We'll explore how language creates rhythm more in the next chapter. For now, keep in mind that readers make meaning. The gaps between scenes, and between chapters, are opportunities for your reader to participate. Think of those gaps as the hallways of your building—spaces where your readers can pause to catch up on their impressions, arrive at conclusions, or compare what they've been reading to their own experiences.

❡

You'll find your own method in creating scenes, in balancing internal and external action, and in developing your story arc. Craft, what we call the Fiction Writer's Toolkit, gives you the tools to do this. Craft, patience, and revision are your greatest assets in building your story. The spotlight exercises above can help you hone your narrative while at the same time allowing you the pleasure of exploring and enjoying the process.

In the next chapter we'll show you how to dress up your scenes and story using vivid language, telling details, description, landscape, and subtext.

5

Painting the Picture
Language and Setting

"We think in generalities," wrote Alfred North Whitehead. "But we live in detail." To which I would add: we remember in detail, we recognize in details, we identify, we re-create—cops rarely ask eyewitnesses for general vague descriptions of the perpetrator.

—FRANCINE PROSE, *Reading Like a Writer: A Guide for People Who Love Books and for Those Who Want to Write Them*

Just as the scene gives your story its power, as we explored in the last chapter, details, particularly telling details, make your story unforgettable. A scene carries us into the action, but details enliven the quality of that action. Think about it: often what you bring away from a book you've read is a striking detail that you can't get out of your mind. The plot may fade, the characters may blend into others, but a colorful detail stays with you forever. In this chapter we'll look at how language—its sensory impact, its construction of a sense of place, and its creation of action—creates those details that make your story memorable.

THE MAGIC OF IMAGERY

One of the most delightful discoveries we make as young readers is the difference between denotative (literal) and connotative (contextual) meanings. While as writers we of course must know a word's denotative meaning, its *possibilities* exist in its connotative qualities, because that's where imagination and the singularity of a writer's voice and style reside.

The *denotative meaning* of a word is its dictionary meaning; the *connotative meaning* includes implied characteristics found in the word's context.

Connotative language makes a word and what it represents personal and specific by removing it from the realm of fact and placing it in the world of imagination. One of the ways the writer connotes meaning is through *imagery*.

Imagery refers to the sensory details of sound, taste, and smell as well as the visual details that provide the reader with an experiential quality.

Imagery imbues language with vitality, while at the same time, as Sue William Silverman notes, "writing our senses helps us remember the past while also allowing us to make sense of it" (71). As humans, we ground our experience in sensory detail, in what something feels like through the range of our five senses. If we're lucky, the sixth sense becomes engaged as well: through vivid writing, the reader begins to intuit aspects of character, plot, and setting.

Using Figurative Language

The basic unit of figurative language is the *metaphor*. When Homer speaks of the "wine-dark sea" in *The Iliad*, he imbues the water with the intensity and bloodshed of war. Denotatively, water is not often "wine dark," but figuratively, the image resonates. As writers, we use metaphors to personalize meaning. When we make the choice to connect two things or sensations via metaphor, we telegraph deeper meaning to the reader.

A *metaphor* connects two unrelated things and creates a relationship between them. The phrase "the chasm of despair," for example, lends an emotional tone and a physical image to an abstract noun.

By making our writing metaphoric, we ask words to behave in specific ways. In *I Could Tell You Stories*, for example, Patricia Hampl, while discussing writing about her childhood piano lessons, seizes on the detail of her red music book: "Now I can look at that music book and see it not only as 'a detail' but for what it is, how it acts. See it as the small red door leading straight into the dark room of my childhood longing and disappointment" (31). Anyone can say her childhood was lonely, but to compare a music book to "the small red door" that leads into longing packs much more power. We want to make our language work hard, to evoke our experience so that someone reading our story who does not know us can *feel* what we're describing.

Related to metaphor is the *symbol*, which refers to a word or concept developed through context and layered by repetition so that it takes on larger meaning. Symbols abound in religious writings and iconography. An example is the cross in the New Testament. By the time we've read about the betrayal, death, and resurrection of Christ, the cross has come to stand as a symbol of both suffering and a path to redemption. Such a symbol becomes familiar and yet retains its meaning in vernacular expression: when we describe someone as "a cross to bear" we convey the idea that the person, and our relationship with him or her, is complex and difficult. Another example is the strong reaction many have to the insignia known as the swastika, evidence that it has continued to be a symbol of intolerance long after the end of World War II.

A *symbol* refers to a word or concept developed through context and layered by repetition so that it takes on larger meaning.

Fairy tales are rich in metaphors and symbols: houses are made of gingerbread and can be eaten, greedy creatures sprout extra arms and legs, and tears heal blind eyes. Because such stories appeal to the imagination and thus the senses, they're peopled with characters and objects that behave like their emotional meaning. For instance, the sense of home nourishes us; a house *built* of food shows that visceral connection. That's the real gift of figurative language: it's automatically both tactile and dramatic, immersing the reader in the experience of the story.

We can look at the workings of a simple metaphor when Willa Cather describes the New Mexico sky in *Death Comes for the Archbishop*: "Elsewhere the sky is the roof of the world; but here the earth was the floor of the sky" (232). By contextualizing things as uncontainable as "world" and "sky" as having a "roof" or a "floor," the metaphor draws a figurative boundary around the bigness. It also firmly implants the notion in the reader's mind of how dominant the sky is—the land grounds its vastness as a floor anchors a room.

If we think of the New Mexico sky as Cather does, as a vast witness to nature and human activity, then we enter the realm of the symbol. A symbol almost always has an ineffable quality, in this case a spiritual connection as well as a physical or descriptive one.

SPOTLIGHT EXERCISES

Reading: Choose a scene from a memoir and identify the kind and quality of metaphoric language used as the protagonist remembers the past or paints a picture for the reader of a specific time or place. What are some specific ways the writer involves you in the sensory images of the scene by using metaphor or symbol? Note any techniques of using figurative language you find compelling that you might use in your story.

Writing: Take one of the scenes you were working on in the exercises in chapter 4, or one of your possible entry points for the occasion of the telling in chapter 1, and experiment with creating metaphors for the action or characters. Use the list below to help you create comparisons that enhance the experiential qualities of your writing. In each case, use figurative writing to connote a sensuous comparison for a feeling, movement, or description.

Animal characteristics: We often compare the qualities or movements of animals to human behavior. Foxes, for example, are thought of as clever, magpies as thieves. Play with the animal characteristics your narrator and characters already possess and see what comes of it.

Color: Many people experience emotional states as colors, and even for those who don't, color imparts mood and tone. What does blue mean to you? Red? Yellow? Are your associations visual? Emotional? Physical? Do you hear certain things when you see certain colors? Try assigning each character in your memoir a color. What color are you?

Texture: Not only have sewing and weaving metaphors come to signify layers and levels of storytelling, but how something feels or looks in three dimensions grabs our attention. How does that blanket, that beach, that cold doorknob *feel*? Show it on the page.

Sound: Auditory cues are a powerful sense for most people, and the earliest stories were spoken aloud rather than written. Use sound to evoke metaphoric feeling—the longing of a train whistle, for example, or the harsh clanging of a locomotive. If you re-create sound effectively on the page, there's no need to name the emotion you're trying to convey, because the auditory cue will serve as metaphor or, perhaps, actually sound like the feeling you're trying to convey (onomatopoeia).

Smell and taste: The most primitive or limbic of our senses, odors, and tastes can resurrect the past. Are there foods that take you back to the first time you tasted them, smells that place you in a moment from your past? Pick one and write about it.

Objects: As Alfred Hitchcock showed us in movies like *Suspicion* (where the glowing glass of possibly poisoned milk in Cary Grant's hand signifies murderous intentions), an object strategically placed can stand in for events or emotional changes and transport us to another moment. Try thinking of an object as fodder for a cinematic quick cut in your memoir and see where it takes you. Even something as simple as a screen door can open (pun intended) into possibility.

LANGUAGE AND SENSE OF PLACE

Telling details and metaphors can help us embellish both the setting and the landscape of our memoirs. Nature writers like Craig Childs and William deBuys, who explore the physical, emotional, and spiritual geography of the American Southwest, utilize language in particularly graphic ways. Setting, where we want to paint pictures for our readers and otherwise immerse them in a scene, gives us great practice with metaphor and *leitmotifs*.

A *leitmotif* is a complex metaphor layered into the story;
it builds associations around a person, place, or thing.

In *The Desert Cries: A Season of Flash Floods in a Dry Land*, Craig Childs describes the Arizona desert using human anatomy as a leitmotif: "The drainages cut into the desert's smooth ground, coalescing into larger and larger arroyos like threads drawn together by a hand. A waist-high forest of creosote bush dominates the vegetation. Gangly arms of ocotillo grow in isolated stands" (15).

Note how the desert in this description is a living organism, its arroyos "like threads drawn together by a hand." The author anthropomorphizes the vegetation: forests are "waist-high," and creosote bush "dominates," while ocotillo has "arms." The sparse vegetation in the shape of human figures takes on the trappings of a *dominant image*, almost as if our minds need to populate the vast land with the illusion of a human presence. The bushes and cacti become spiritual witnesses that counter the emptiness.

One important benefit of writing about place is that doing so particularizes your story: each place is specific, with telling characteristics. The best nonfiction writing personalizes and characterizes; objects—as well as natural forms of earth and rock, plants, and animals—come alive as unique characters. As Childs illustrates, vivid nature writing doesn't merely list details about setting, it *animates* them. Similarly, a strong setting doesn't just anchor your story; it also imbues it with a living context that allows you, its author, to layer its meaning.

In a related example, Childs uses the *sustaining metaphor* of river imagery as he describes a thunderstorm: "The thunderstorm first boils into southern Nevada. Balls of hail 2 inches wide blanket Las Vegas. Then the water comes, flooding the streets. Cars are thrown into each other like reckless barges, scraping sideways along medians. Tropicana Avenue becomes a river 50 feet wide. In the middle of this avenue, a fire truck drives in, acting as a dam to protect a stranded car" (99).

Dominant images and *sustaining metaphors* gather momentum as the story moves forward, like the proverbial snowball rolling down the hill. Through accretion of key images and metaphors, mood and tone are set by the writer and communicated to the reader. See also *scaffolding* in chapter 3.

Childs compares rain with the power and force of a mighty river, using words like "boils" and "flooding." Cars are helpless in the storm, "thrown into each other like reckless barges," so that a rescue vehicle acts "as a dam." These descriptions add an agency and urgency to a simple rainstorm, dramatizing it as a ferocious force of nature.

In *The Walk*, a testimonial to the New Mexico spirit and landscape, William deBuys describes standing in a forest after an apocalyptic burn and contemplating its cycles of growth and destruction: "Here I stand in a forest riven with illness, out of balance, disordered, a place of problems. Yet it is undeniably a delight to the senses.... The caress it offers may be the touch of the misshapen hand, but the caress is no less delicate, sensuous, and welcome. The forest asks us to love what is marred. It shows us the scarred face of beauty, the smile of broken teeth" (29).

In this excerpt deBuys builds a leitmotif of nature as a lover; his experience, which he invites us to join in, dramatizes the natural world as an intimate familiar.

Setting as Metaphor

As we discussed in chapter 3, a strong setting for your story makes organic sense in the same way that the right structure does: it cements the disparate sections of your story together. In poet Rachel Hadas's memoir, *Strange Relation*, the decline of the narrator's husband, George, is inextricably linked to the New York City landscape. When George takes a different route to his tennis match in Central Park, deviating from habits the narrator has witnessed for thirty years, it marks a turning point for her in his progressing dementia: "The new route involved less than one extra block to walk to get to the park. Still, this unexplained change in route and routine made no sense to me. We'd always gone the other, shorter way; and harmony lay precisely in habit. The fabric of our days was woven from routine" (105).

When it is eloquent, we often compare gesture to poetry in motion. But, always, as we write and weave together place and character, the body in space is revealing as well as poetic.

Sometimes, in addition to serving as landscape and grounding, the setting takes on symbolic meaning and transcends place, giving us details of milieu and of mood as well as mere location. For example, Annie Dillard's Pittsburgh is not just a city and its environs but a place during a specific era, the 1950s of her growing up. At the beginning of *An American Childhood*, Dillard tells the reader that when everything else is gone from her brain, Pittsburgh's topography will still trigger specific yearnings and memories in her psyche. This symbolic landscape re-creates an epic representation of childhood as a state of being and the past as a magical place, the city animated by embellished memories.

Dillard's Pennsylvania setting in *An American Childhood* provides the ground for her imagination to manifest itself. In this way, place is inseparable from experience. Humans ground experience not in a vacuum but rather in a specific place. Because the memoir is in part an exercise in resurrecting a specific past, setting is therefore integral to the scaffolding of its meaning. Metaphorical detail about place encapsulates the memoir's episodes for the reader: place locates experience.

Place as Time Period

Since place and time period are so intertwined, often specifics of place are metaphoric of *milieu* as well. While both *The Year of Magical Thinking* and *The Liars' Club* partly take place in the 1970s and 1980s, they are very different. Didion gives the reader scores of details not only about her life in New York City but also about the qualities of an urban artist and intellectual who occupies a particular social, professional, and economic sphere. The details of people, restaurants, events, and travel pinpoint an era and interlocking subcultures of class and taste as well as place. Contrast this with Mary Karr's book, which captures a rural, southern, working-class culture.

Milieu refers to the social environment and often the ambience of a setting. It can reference a historical time as well as the values of an era or an author.

SPOTLIGHT EXERCISES

Reading: Choose a memoir and record your impressions of how details of place affect the action and mood in one or more chapters. How do details of landscape highlight certain experiences in the memoir? Are there images that recur and acquire symbolic power? How is that achieved? List aspects of social and cultural environment that are also revealed.

Writing: Create a visual representation for a sequence in your story: on a large piece of paper, map where the key events in your story occur. Insert images or metaphors that bring the place to life. Feel free to draw pictures and circle words. You may want to visually trace the connections between your various characters or graph the arc of the plot as well. In this way, you may discover a key setting where your story comes together or pulls apart. In any case, you'll discover new correspondences by activating your visual sense with the physicality of drawing and writing.

LANGUAGE AS ACTION

We usually think of action as something occurring in the physical world—a body falling off a cliff, a tank rolling through the countryside, a gun going off. Yet much of the movement in your story comes through the way you use language to create the rhythm of events by evoking either the movement of time, the real-time action of dialogue, or the quality of silence.

Controlling Time

We mentioned time in the memoir in chapter 4 during our discussion of rising action in scene and plot. In this section, we'll show how you can use language to control the experience of time, or duration, through *scene, summary,* and *description*. The emphasis you place on various happenings in your story, highlighting and extending some sequences while glossing over others, allows you to control the movement of time in your memoir.

Both summary and description lead us back to kairos, the holy time we mentioned in chapter 4. Kairos exists in the narrator's *perception* of events, as opposed to the literal "facts" of the plot, and therefore determines the emphasis of the story. For example, if a writer says something like "The first ten years of my life were inconsequential," she is minimizing that time in her life. Alternately, if a writer spends a hundred pages on the moment when the narrator realizes his life has changed, let's say on the death of a loved one, he signals to the reader that this elongated moment has much importance.

A *scene* takes place in actual time. Because it contains largely
dialogue with minimal reaction, the pacing of a scene reflects the
amount of time that such an interchange might actually take.

A *summary* is a collapsing of time, as in "four years later . . ."
The writer makes a transition to let the reader know where he or
she is in time, but the brief mention of time is vastly shorter
than the chronicling of "four years" or whatever chunk of time
the writer is referencing.

A *description* expands time. The writer may linger on a moment
that in the thinking could be a flash but that in the telling is
leisurely. Description arrests time and allows for psychological
detail as well.

As the perception of actual time in scene is familiar to us both from daily
life and from scenes in film and onstage, we'll use the trope of film to look
more closely at summary and description in Mira Bartók's award-winning
memoir, *The Memory Palace*. First, the narrator summarizes one year of her
life after an accident when she says: "For the rest of the year I wear a black
patch over my left eye. It isn't easy to see. I run into furniture and trip over my
feet. At home, in our apartment, I pretend I am blind" (35). Because the telling
moment in that year for the narrator is her eye injury, the patch becomes the
symbol of this time.

The narrator then recounts a moment during her recovery when her mad
mother, who believes she is alone, races around the living room, stumbling
and talking to herself. At first the narrator thinks her mother is just imitating
Crazy Guggenheim, a favorite television character of the 1960s. But then her
mother appears to become someone else, so terrifying the narrator, who is
still in kindergarten, that time appears to stretch infinitely, an attribute that
descriptive language can capture:

Suddenly my mother turns into someone else, someone I can't recognize from
TV. She makes slicing movements in the air. She's holding something now,
something long and shiny. She spins around fast as if someone has just crept up
behind her. She is spinning and spinning, obscenities rolling off her tongue,
words I've only heard my grandfather use. There is the smell of burnt toast and
cigarettes, no music coming from anywhere, no radio or TV. . . . I don't know
how it ends, this scene—the beginning of knowledge, the knowledge that I have
a secret I must keep from the outside world. In this scene, my mother is forever

spinning, wielding a knife. . . . She is forever spinning and I am forever watching her with my one good eye—a small child frozen behind a wall. (37)

During this sequence, where the reader shares with the narrator the sense of being frozen in time, sensory details also arrest the action into a tableau: the visual imagery of the spinning and spinning and the movement of the knife, the smells of burnt toast and cigarettes, the sound of cursing and yet the absence of sound from the radio or TV (the narrator has told us the radio always plays). Even the image of the child watching with one eye conveys an impression and colors the bizarreness of the scene almost in the way that a fish-eye lens distorts our sense of time and reality. The description, the sense of time stopping, and the sensory images all lend a surrealistic air to the moment.

Dialogue

In addition to creating a sense of actual time, dialogue can also capture character and *tone*. As writers we want to discern the differences in the word choices our characters use to show their emotional states, the qualities they have as people, and the color and mood, or tone, of a scene. Nothing reveals character more quickly than the particular way people speak.

Tone refers to the overall mood of a story or a scene. It is the emotional coloring a writer creates through language, events, and rhythm.

Dialogue tells us what people pay attention to and, therefore, what their motives and priorities are. In addition, how people talk contains the seeds of the way they think. The modernist writer Gertrude Stein wrote in the 1930s about how the complete person is revealed by the repetition of their speech: "I began to get enormously interested in hearing how everybody said the same thing over and over again with infinite variations but over and over again until finally if you listened with great intensity you could hear it rise and fall and tell all that that there was inside them, not so much by the actual words they said or the thoughts they had but the movement of their thoughts and words endlessly the same and endlessly different" (138).

In dialogue, word choice (*diction*) and the arrangement of words (*syntax*) say as much about a character as the content or implication of what he or she is saying. Dialogue reveals each character's motives through either what the person says or what he or she omits.

In a sentence or utterance, *diction* refers to the choice of words and style of enunciation. *Syntax* refers to the arrangement of the words in a sentence or utterance.

While many memoirs are longer on description and telling by the first-person narrator, others employ dialogue, particularly in scene, to marvelous effect. In *Eat, Pray, Love,* Elizabeth Gilbert uses dialogue to establish the character of Richard from Texas. His insouciance and commonsense approach to life come out in his speech:

> "What's got you all wadded up?" he drawls, toothpick in mouth, as usual.
> "Don't ask," I say . . ."And worst of all, I can't stop obsessing over David. I thought I was over him, but it's all coming up again."
> He says, "Give it another six months, you'll feel better."
> "I've already given it twelve months, Richard."
> "Then give it six more. Just keep throwin' six months at it till it goes away. Stuff like this takes time." (148)

Richard's colorful way of speaking, with a touch of Texan in both word choice and rhythm ("wadded up," "keep throwin' six months at it"), nonetheless dramatizes his casual, no-nonsense approach to life. At the same time, it contrasts with Liz's naive earnestness and stubborn reasonableness ("I've already given it twelve months, Richard"). And both characters' dialogue emphasizes the humor of the situation and therefore reinforces tone. *Eat, Pray, Love* became a best seller partly because of its combination of tragicomedy and whimsy about one of life's most common plots: woman needing to change her life drastically divorces her husband and goes on a quest to find herself. But it also owes much of its success to Gilbert's ability to use dialogue to reveal character.

This brief snippet of dialogue also shows us strongly the sense of *relationship* between these two characters: they are so comfortable with one another that they can be completely direct. Their language is casual, not formal, indicating familiarity: they pull no punches. Dialogue can therefore show closeness or, if one character uses more formal language than the other, create distance. For example, if during an argument one person says, "You're unfair to me," and the other responds, "To what do you refer?," the second person's formal diction pushes the first person away. The use of elevated diction is also a play to establish dominance over the first speaker. There are, of course, many ways that dialogue, or the lack of it, can show distance.

Sometimes a single line of dialogue can define a character. In Oscar Hijuelos's memoir, *Thoughts without Cigarettes*, the narrator listens to his father, who was born in Cuba, talk about the death of his brother: "He was my life, and my blood, who taught me everything I know" (64). From this one sentence we absorb the father's tone of nostalgia as well as his heartfelt grief. The father, a character slightly bigger than life to the narrator, speaks dramatically, but at the same his diction and syntax suggest the Spanish rhythms of his background, including a more formal tone than colloquial American speech.

Silence

As anyone who appreciates the dramatic work of Samuel Beckett or Harold Pinter can attest, silence plays powerfully onstage. In Beckett's *Waiting for Godot* and Pinter's *Betrayal*, the meaning and implication of the drama come *between the lines*, or in the pauses between the characters' lines.

This is of course true in actual life as well. Think of an argument or a conflict you've recently been involved in and you'll realize how little of each person's issues are actually revealed in detail by what he or she said. Body language plays a big part, as does Stein's comment above about repetition. One person might say, "You don't listen to me," over and over, while the other repeats, "Tell me what's wrong." But especially in times of high emotion, people often say very little. The real tremors happen under the surface.

An exception to the "tip of the iceberg" theory comes when a character is intellectual or very articulate; in this case, that character's very volubility may disguise discomfort. In addition, the way people speak in stressful situations often shows whether they first respond mentally or physically. For example, in *The Glass Castle*, the narrator, a bright and precocious child, has just moved to a new school in the fifth grade and has been mistakenly put in a class for students with learning disabilities. Her teacher refers to her by telling the class that some people think they're so special, they don't have to follow the rules. When the instructor asks the class, "Who thinks that's not fair?," everyone but the narrator raises an arm in the air. When the teacher calls upon the narrator to explain herself, she attempts to dazzle the group by saying: "Insufficient information to draw a conclusion" (138). Her brainy response backfires and makes her more of an object of ridicule than she was before.

It's one thing to establish mood or move a scene through dialogue or description and another to slow the rhythm to a standstill. Writers often establish a sense of silence in memoir by creating space. Patti Smith accomplishes this toward the end of her memoir, *Just Kids*, when she realizes that she will soon lose Robert. One day, when they are alone, he says to her: "Patti, I'm dying. It's so painful." Patti helps him to the couch and sits with him until he falls asleep. As she thinks of how unendurable his life has become, she thinks: "The light poured through the windows upon his photographs and the poem of us sitting together a last time. Robert dying: creating silence. Myself, destined to live, listening closely to a silence that would take a lifetime to express" (276).

In this case, Smith uses description that gives the impression of cessation. She lets us feel time shutting down, thought shutting down, and thereby allows us to experience this long moment during which they exist side by side. By listening so closely to this moment herself, the reader too stops and listens. Smith envelops the moment in silence.

Another writer may focus on the natural world to convey silence, narrowing the reader's focus until he feels an opportunity for meditation along with the narrator. Here is William deBuys looking at the Swimming Hole,

SPOTLIGHT EXERCISES

Reading: From the memoir you chose in the last spotlight exercise on setting, isolate passages that show action in ways that highlight psychological action as opposed to physical action. For example, look at how the narrator's reflections move the story along in a particular scene. How does word choice play a part in addition to rhythm and mood?

Writing: Construct a scene using only dialogue between two characters. How can you show each character listening as well as talking? How can the dialogue show relationship? Conflict?

Reading and writing: Explore a moment of silence in a memoir of your choosing. How does the author use words, the lack of words, rhythm, or repetition to convey silence or cessation of time? Now imagine a silent moment in your story and construct three versions, one using gesture only, one using description, and the last using rhythm and/or repetition. Which example most fully telegraphs your intention?

a pool in the Río de las Trampas, the river of traps: "The other current does not escape the pool. The farther half of the onrushing stream pours crashing in, but the standing waves shoulder it aside. It veers and turns on itself. It gyres into a deep, froth-topped eddy, dark and cold, that cycles and circles, round and round, corkscrewing inexorably to the black, down-sucking center. I stare into it transfixed. The eddy spirals and spins. . . . I see in the eddy the embodiment of irresolution—everything pulled round in a cold circle, nothing escaping" (51). In this passage, deBuys creates an infinity of movement that nonetheless stops time. The narrator can only stare, mesmerized and immobilized. Both Smith and deBuys employ repetition and rhythm to paradoxically create stillness.

By examining these sequences that show "time out of mind," we observe the elasticity of language and its ability to construct action across a wide spectrum. Whether the action is physical, emotional, psychological, or spiritual, it requires its own vocabulary and rhythm.

The Secrets of Subtext

Action in a story is sometimes overt and at other times covert. The hidden meanings you may have found when analyzing dialogue in the exercise above reveal the layerings of story we call *subtext*. It takes a book to uncover all the marvelous possibilities of subtext, and for that purpose we refer you to Charles Baxter's *The Art of Subtext*. As Baxter explains, "You put in the foreground, the staging area, the story that is going on now. This story gradually reveals what has happened in the past, where the chronic tensions are, and whose echoes are still audible" (26).

> *Subtext* exists beneath the surface of the story and is shown
> via detail, dialogue, and scene, revealing (in Charles Baxter's
> words) its "chronic tensions."

Subtext is a particularly powerful tool in the writing of a memoir because a memoir's power often resides in the unwrapping of those chronic tensions. "Denial battles with desire every day" (72), Baxter tells us, and "sometimes, what you don't hear tells [us] more than what you actually say" (81).

A searing example of subtext can be found in Linda Gray Sexton's *Searching for Mercy Street*. Gray's mother, poet Anne Sexton, asks the nine-year-old Linda to pretend that she is thirty-four, Sexton's age at the time, so that Anne can pretend she is nine. The subtext beneath the dialogue here is harrowing: How could a mother carry such a "game" so far?

> "Could you be thirty-four now?"
> "Pretty soon," [Anne] promises. . . .
> "Mommy?" I plead. "Please?"
> "No," she pouts. "I'm nine."
> "Please," I say and start to sob, my chest heaving its burden up and down.
> "I'm nine!"
> "Please be thirty-four!"
> "I can't be thirty-four—I'm just a little girl. I'm *your* little girl. Don't you want me anymore?" (59)

In this scene, the mother's actions and words show her abdicating her mothering role. The scene is a microcosm of the relationship of mother and daughter. As the memoir establishes over and over again, Anne Sexton desperately wanted her eldest daughter to take care of her, pushing Linda Gray Sexton into the role of parent. It was a role she had no training for, particularly at the age of nine.

Subtext can also be revealed via detail and gesture: a character may say one thing and accompany that statement with a gesture that tells the reader he means something else entirely—without the narrator explaining to the reader. One of the beauties of subtext is that it requires us to participate as readers: we must make the decision about the meaning of the contradiction and what the narrator is showing us. Readers are eager to fill in the gaps, to see through characters long before the characters themselves understand their underlying motivations. The writer's construction of subtext in her story—part of the scaffolding of meaning we've talked about before—encourages the reader to be part of the story. Involvement increases the reader's commitment to your story.

In this chapter we've explored ways of highlighting place, time, rhythm, and mood. While language creates action, details provide the momentum and the lasting impression for the reader. As Francine Prose reminds us, "Details aren't only the building blocks with which a story is put together, they're also clues to something deeper, keys not merely to our subconscious but to our historical moment" (207).

In the next chapter we'll look at how writers establish a compelling voice and style and show how you can develop a voice and style uniquely your own.

6

Your Story, Your Voice
Make It Your Own

> Maybe a reader's love of memoir is less an intrusive lust for confession
> than a hankering for the intimacy of [the] first-person voice, the deeply
> satisfying sense of being spoken to privately. More than a story, we want
> a voice speaking softly, urgently, in our ear.
>
> —PATRICIA HAMPL, *I Could Tell You Stories: Sojourns in the
> Land of Memory*

Every writer has her own unique style and voice, and in memoir this style and
voice inform the story being told as the author views her remembered self
with compassion, humor, and even forgiveness. As Patricia Hampl notes
above, readers yearn for connection via the intimacy of the first-person voice.
Just as with a close friend, the quality of the voice in your ear is one of the
reasons people read to begin with: that voice can nurture, entertain, provoke
wisdom, and provide companionship. So it follows that developing an authentic voice of your own is one of the most important tools you'll master as you
write your memoir.

In this chapter we'll explore some of the voices and styles used in a variety of memoirs, including memoirs by writers known in other genres. We'll
also delineate the difference between you, the narrator, and you, the character—yet another aspect of the two yous. Finally, we'll give you some important tools from the Fiction Writer's Toolkit to help you hone your own voice
and style.

THE FIRST-PERSON VOICE

Discovering the right voice for your memoir means more than simply writing
down what you remember. It means finding the voice that can best tell *this*
story, *now*.

We emphasize "this" story because every memoir demands a specialized,
nuanced "you." Memoirs are almost always related in the first-person singular,

since it's your "I" that is both telling and living the story. Open any memoir to its first page, and you'll find that "I," that intimate, confiding, first-person voice that figuratively takes your hand and invites you into the story, as Lynn Freed does in *Reading, Writing, and Leaving Home*: "Only long after I was old enough to read for myself, did I really make the connection between literature and the printed word. My mother . . . preferred to tell her own versions of the stories that other parents read to their children. . . . This way she could add characters at will, eliminate others, change the plot around, and thus string out the story into a series of episodic cliff-hangers" (1–2).

> *Voice* refers to the sound of the narrator on the page. More nuanced and sophisticated than your regular speaking voice, your voice on the page is the you who can best tell *this* story.

Because Freed's memoir's focus is her development as a writer, it makes sense that its occasion of the telling is her earliest experience of storytelling. But listen to the voice here—it's not the young child's but rather that of Freed the writer. Freed establishes this in her first three words: "Only long after." Even as she returns to her experiencing self, her voice here is one of experience and knowledge—a remembering narrator, important in this memoir because Freed uses her experience to teach what she has learned about writing.

Between Experience and Remembering

How a voice sounds on the page depends, first, on the story being told and, second, on how you the author choose to tell it. As Sue William Silverman notes in *Fearless Confessions*, "The voice of each piece you write needs its own tone, rhythm, vocabulary, and energy" (51).

The first-person voice you choose for your memoir will move between the experiencing you and the remembering you we discussed in chapter 2. Here, for example, is Terry Tempest Williams in *Refuge: An Unnatural History of Family and Place*: "I have refused to believe that Mother will die. And by denying her cancer, even her death, I deny her life. Denial stops us from listening. I cannot hear what Mother is saying. I can only hear what I want" (75–76).

Notice how Williams moves from the experiencing self in the first sentence to the remembering self in the rest of the paragraph. Even though *Refuge* is written in the present tense, it's the remembering self who judges the experiencing self and finds her wanting. In the sentence "Denial stops us from listening," Williams has stepped even farther back by employing first-person *plural*. She then returns to the experiencing self after the remembering self has rendered this judgment. Note that, despite the insight of the remembering self, the experiencing self has not changed. She still "only hear[s] what [she] want[s]."

SPOTLIGHT EXERCISE

Writing: If you've written at all, you already know your writing voice sounds different from your speaking voice. For this exercise, you'll need a recording device (your computer or phone may well have one). Pick a story from your past you know well, perhaps one that you've told many times but have never written down. Without any preparation (no time for worry—just do it!), record the story, with the understanding that no one but you will ever listen to this recording. You're recording it only for the purpose of this exercise.

Don't play back the recording immediately after you've made it. Instead, move on to the next step in this exercise and write down the story. You may find yourself crossing things out (or, if you're typing, deleting them) as well as moving words or even sentences around. That's fine—this is the written version, and that's precisely what writers do. Take your time, perhaps even going back to polish your draft the next day.

When you've finished this written draft, print out a hard copy. Now comes the point of all this. Have one or more colored pens or pencils ready, then play back the recording. Using different colors for different nuances (red for word choice, for example, or blue for elision or expansion), note where what's on the page differs from what you say in the recording.

Next, consider the differences between these two versions. Are there different word choices—"lovely" instead of "awesome," for example? Did you phrase your sentences more formally or reorder the telling to enhance its effect? Did you, like Williams, shift into another person to make a point? Maybe in the written version you chose to give more detail about a particular moment or realized that another moment didn't need to be there at all. Each of these differences between your spoken voice and your written one is a hallmark of your writing voice. Practicing the hallmarks you discover in this exercise can help you make your writer's voice still stronger and more distinct.

Beyond First Person

While first person is a given for the bulk of memoir, some of the more intriguing selections we've found are written in the third (he or she) or even the second (you) person. Shifting between persons within a narrative is an acquired skill, but there are a number of occasions where it can work to your advantage. You might, for example, find it difficult to write about a particular traumatic moment from your past, like this instance from Hilda Raz's memoir *What Becomes You*, written with her son, Aaron Raz Link, a transgendered male who was born Hilda's daughter, Sarah: "How does a mother enter the heart and skin of a human being not herself, a boy/girl she 'grew in her center like the very air'? Can she?" (251).

Raz's use of the third person here offers her, the writer, the perspective she needs to bring to life her difficulty with the fact that Sarah has become Aaron. Raz, who has a distinguished career specializing in literature and gender studies, shifts the moment closer to readers through its vivid language. Raz moves between first and third person in order to negotiate the difficulty she has with navigating a gender issue so close to home. In this case, the intentional distancing of third person conversely allows Raz to acknowledge that difficulty and to move closer to the reader. The way memoir writers negotiate life's most difficult challenges, as we've pointed out, keeps readers engaged. Just as when we're arguing with ourselves in our heads, the memoir writer uses different voices—in this case moving from first to third person.

Abigail Thomas employs second person to similar effect in *Safekeeping: Some True Stories from a Life*. In fact, Thomas moves among first, second, and third person throughout this unusual memoir, a pastiche of memory that ultimately serves as a moving tribute to her recently deceased second husband. Here's the opening of one such second-person section: "For him love/marriage was a fencing match; you never allowed your opponent the upper hand. Your mate was your opponent, although it was all in good fun. You never revealed your vulnerable spot, but you went after theirs with the lightest of touches" (57).

In this passage both Thomas and her husband might be "you," a conceit that shows that both were equally adept at the "fencing matches" that characterized their marriage. To understand why this works, imagine the passage in first person instead: "Love/marriage was a fencing match for both of us; neither of us allowed his or her opponent the upper hand." Even this quick change of person in the passage's first sentence shows that, for Thomas's purposes, while first person would distance the reader from the moment (or, in this case, moments), second moves the reader *into* it.

It's important to emphasize that, for the most part, first person is the logical choice for sharing your own story—it allows the writer to go inside her own story and dig deeply into the self. We offer these examples only as a possible method for you to reveal moments for which first person doesn't seem to work or for which you need the distance of second or third person to connect with the reader or to explore complex issues at a greater remove.

SPOTLIGHT EXERCISES

Reading: Analyze a section from one of the books mentioned in this chapter and reflect on how the use of first, second, or third person affects your involvement as a reader.

Writing: One of the advantages of writing about your experiencing self in the third person is that it can help you approach material you've found difficult to write about until now. For this exercise, select an embarrassing moment from your past—preferably something you've never shared with anyone. Next, give the experiencing you a name—make her a character, in other words. Finally, create a scene for that character, using the embarrassing moment as its basis. Allow what really happened *and your emotions* about the scene—both then and now—free rein on the page. After all, you're not writing about *you* anymore but about your *character*.

When you've finished, put the scene away until the next day. When you do read the piece, see if you've gotten closer to the character-you (and his emotions) by using the third person. We'll bet you have. Writing in the third person allows us to approach problematic moments that are even now difficult to acknowledge.

If this is a scene that your memoir needs, you can now rewrite it using the first person. Or you may choose to keep it in third person or even experiment with second. The important thing is to get every scene that's intrinsic to your story on the page. Changing person can help you do so.

Your Two Voices

Just as we refer to a novel's narrator and a poem's speaker, we like to differentiate between the author of a memoir and the character of the author within it when we talk about the work itself. This partly harks back to the two yous, but in this case, we'd like you to think of the two yous as you, the narrator, and you, the character.

You, the Narrator

As you discovered in the exercise above, where you recorded a scene, then wrote it down, the narrator you is not really you but rather a literary construction you create to tell a particular story. She won't have your speaking voice but rather an enhanced voice that can approach the material with both wisdom and style. As Sue William Silverman puts it, "The 'I' in memoir is a literary device to both enhance and explore complicated truths" (53).

In addition, the you who narrates your memoir is not only the remembering you or the experiencing you but rather a combination of both. It's through your voice that you'll move back and forth between these two yous, weaving a coherent and compelling story that captures your readers.

Thinking of yourself as a narrator can be enormously freeing. This is why one of the things writing teachers usually discourage in the writing workshop is the use of the second person when talking about another's work-in-progress, as in, "When you kill the bad guy on page 7 . . ." Most likely (we hope!), the author hasn't killed the bad guy, on page 7 or anywhere else; a character—perhaps even the protagonist—has. It's for this reason that we insist on separating author from character—*even in memoir*. The literary term *implied author* helps remind us that there is a creator behind every work.

Implied author refers to the imagined person behind the narrative voice of a work as opposed to the actual author of that work. The implied author is created, just as the work itself is.

We mention this term here because you might think of the implied author as the voice you use to tell a particular story. Understanding that even your memoir has an implied author can help provide the narrative distance you need to tell your story in a compelling way. In addition, as we mentioned earlier in this book, the self does not stand still. The you writing your story now has grown and changed from the you who experienced the story. Separating the narrator from yourself makes that distinction easier to navigate as well.

While the implied author is a construct from literary criticism, the delineation between you, the writer, and you, the storyteller, comes from the Fiction Writer's Toolkit and so may be an even more easily understood construct to grasp. You might think of the writer as the physical you, the one sitting at the keyboard typing now, at this moment, and the storyteller as the you on the page, both living and reliving moments as they unfold there. Sue William Silverman likes to call these two voices "the voice of experience" and "the voice of innocence" (51).

Throughout her memoir, *Stealing Buddha's Dinner*, Bich Minh Nguyen negotiates the line between the writer and the storyteller (or, as Silverman defines them, the voice of experience and the voice of innocence), as she does here, in the book's opening sentences: "We arrived in Grand Rapids with five dollars and a knapsack of clothes. Mr. Heidenga, our sponsor, set us up with a rental house, some groceries . . . and gave us dresses his daughters had outgrown. He hired my father to work a filling machine at North American Feather. Mr. Heidenga wore wide sport coats and had yellow hair" (1).

Nguyen's memoir is about moving (or, more aptly, escaping) to Michigan from Vietnam in 1975, when she was a very young girl. The first two sentences here are in the writer's voice, as the scene is set through narrative. Then there is a transition sentence from the writer to the storyteller, who then tells us in the last sentence quoted here that "Mr. Heidenga wore wide sport coats and had yellow hair." Where Nguyen the writer might have embellished this sentence, the very young storyteller tells us, from her child point of view, what she sees. The young storyteller, the experiencing self, is "innocent," as she doesn't have the distance or judgment that the reminiscent self has.

For another example, we look to Margaret Atwood's story collection *Moral Disorder: Stories* (which we've chosen to cite because the author acknowledges that this book is as autobiographical as anything she's ever written), in which Atwood dances between writer and storyteller just as we've come to expect of this celebrated writer of fiction and poetry. In this scene, the narrator's much-younger sister has demanded she impersonate a monster, one of the sister's favorite games that nonetheless terrifies her: "'All right,' I'd say, though I was quite sure how it would end. 'I'll count to ten. Then I'm coming to get you.' I said this last in my flat monster voice. By the time I'd reached ten, my sister would already have shut herself in the front hall closet with the winter coats and the vacuum cleaner, and would be calling in a muffled voice, 'The game's over! The game's over!'" (38).

Atwood the narrator here chooses the conditional tense—I *would* say, I *would be* calling—while Atwood the storyteller pulls us into the scene with the dialogue and the description of that front hall closet. Atwood is such a skilled writer that her zigzagging back and forth between voices is invisible to the reader—and renders the scene vivid on the page.

You, the Character

Some of us can point to clear delineators in our lives, with the result that we have come to regard the child, teenager, or young adult we once were as if he or she were someone other than ourselves. Applying that perspective to the you in your memoir can help you find the right voice to tell your story. Put another way, regarding your past self (or selves) as someone other than your current self offers an added layer of understanding. The separation this affords allows you to see the story elements in your past and releases you somewhat from the pressure of trying to recall *what factually happened.*

One of Lisa's students, Marcia Sargent, went further, insisting that early drafts of her memoir *Wing Wife: How to Be Married to a Fighter Pilot* were fiction. When, at Lisa's urging, Marcia went back and turned this thinly veiled autobiographical coming-of-age novel into the memoir it was meant to be, the perspective—and depth—gained by writing the story first as fiction was a decided advantage to the character of the experiencing self in the book.

Marcia had been relatively young and undeniably naive when she'd married her Marine fighter pilot husband. Here she is, for example, about to attend her first squadron gathering:

> I touched Andy on the arm. "Will they like me?"
> He patted my hand and smiled down at me. "Of course they'll like you."
> Doubt slithered deeper in my abdomen. No "of course" about it. I didn't even know if *I* liked me. Why should anyone else enjoy having me around? (3)

Even if we've never been in a similar situation, even in the unlikely event that we've never lacked confidence, we as readers nonetheless feel an immediate identification with Marcia, the character—the young wife who's unsure of herself—because of the honesty of emotion in the voice here. That's what you're after when you write about you, the character—a sincere voice that connects with readers.

VOICES OF THE MASTERS

We recognize writers' voices through their particular usage of language, or style. *Style* is one of those tools in the Fiction Writer's Toolkit that's most easily defined by example. So rather than give you long speeches about various aspects of style, we've chosen to let a number of brilliant stylists speak for themselves by discussing memoirs by Mary Karr, Eudora Welty, Mario Vargas Llosa, Margaret Atwood, and Mary Oliver.

Style refers to the sound of the voice on the page: its tone, rhythm, and way of speaking.

In the sections that follow, we'll unpack each writer's particular tools and show you how they combine to create his or her unique style.

"She Opened Herself Up a Worm Farm"

If we were to point to one single aspect of Mary Karr's writing that has made each of her successive memoirs such a success, it would have to be her winning style. Karr on the page is often a wisecracking smart-ass, her language crackling, direct, and, often, hysterically funny. Here's an example from *The Liars' Club*. Karr's Uncle Frank has appeared unexpectedly to pick up Mary and her sister Leica from school:

> Uncle Frank kneeled down eye-level to tell me that Grandma had "passed away." I remember this phrase seemed an unnaturally polite way of putting it, like something you'd hear on *Bonanza*. All the local terms for dying started more or less coursing through my head right then. *She bought the farm, bit the big one, cashed in her chips,* and my favorite: *she opened herself up a worm farm.* (I had the smug pleasure once of using this term up north and having a puzzled young banker-to-be then ask me if these worm farmers in Texas sold worms for fishing, or what.) (99)

With her inimitable voice and conversational style, Karr can't resist not only cracking wise but also offering the reader an aside from her remembering self that makes light of the moment despite its difficulty. Notice how Karr uses both the phrasings of her East Texas childhood and a cultural signpost that serves as a time marker to render this scene vivid. Before she catalogs "the local terms for dying," she tells us that they "more or less" occurred to her "right then." Both of these latter phrasings are themselves hallmarks of Karr's voice—down-home and downright funny and so, by extension, honest—a voice the reader trusts.

"The Fortuneteller Was Not Guilty"

Before you go thinking that wisecracking is a hallmark of southern style, let's take a look at the lovely, wise voice of Eudora Welty. While it's true Welty can be wickedly funny (if you haven't read her classic "Why I Live at the P.O.," we encourage you to stop reading right this minute and do so), her humor emerges not from the wisecrack or quick rejoinder but rather from the characters themselves. Here, in *One Writer's Beginnings*, she relates a tale about her mother's attorney father, Ned Andrews, in which Ned defends a fortuneteller who predicts a man's death and then is accused of his murder when the man is found dead of a gunshot wound in his bed the next day:

> Ned Andrews' defense centered on the well-known fact that the old man kept his loaded gun mounted at all times over the head of his bed. This was the gun that had shot him. The old man could have discharged it perfectly easily himself, Ned argued, by carelessly bouncing on the bed a little bit. He proposed to prove it, and led the jury of dubious mountaineers to watch him do it. Leading them all the way up the mountain to the old man's cabin, he mounted the gun in place on its rests, having first loaded it with blank shells, and while they watched he mimicked the old man and made a running jump onto the bed. The gun jarred loose, tumbled down, and fired at him. He rested his case. The fortuneteller was without any more ado declared not guilty. (52–53)

Notice here how Welty lets her character carry the story. Yes, it's being told by a third-person narrator (Welty herself), but Ned's cleverness is revealed *through the details of the story itself.* She shows Ned to be thorough and rather courtly too in this excerpt. Unlike Karr's down-home style, Welty employs a sage storyteller who uses an enhanced version of the language of her particular place (Mississippi) to render the story vivid to the reader.

"Reveal[ing] Those Demons That Obsess Him"

Award-winning Peruvian novelist Mario Vargas Llosa's *A Writer's Reality* pulls back the curtain on some of the real-life moments that precipitated his novels. As Vargas Llosa puts it, "The novelist . . . reveals those demons that obsess him—his nostalgia, his guilt, sometimes his resentment. . . . The personal experiences that were the first stimulus to write the novel are so insidiously disguised during the process of creation that when the novel is finished, no one, often not even the novelist himself, can easily hear that autobiographical heart that inevitably beats in all fiction" (57).

Vargas Llosa's stance here is of the teacher, which is why he assumes a third-person, authoritative voice to explain his own process. But even when he moves into first person to show "those demons that obsess him," Vargas Llosa retains this self-referential distance as he circles closer and closer to when, as a nine-year-old boy, his family moved to Piura, a time about which he still obsesses. "My mother says that the reason is that that year I saw the sea for the first time" (58), Vargas Llosa tells us first, going into some historical depth regarding this theory before suggesting: "The main reason that my stay in Piura affected me so deeply was that in that year some of my friends, in an afternoon when we tried to swim in the almost dead waters of the Piura River, told me something that constituted an emotional earthquake for me: that babies did not come from Paris, that it was not true that white storks brought them to life from exotic regions" (59).

Let's pause here to compare Mario Vargas Llosa's style with that of Mary Karr and Eudora Welty. Karr, as we noted, assumes a jaunty vernacular that lends her narrative sass. Welty offers a discerning and shrewd narrator who allows the character to reveal the story. Vargas Llosa's style resembles neither of these. The phrasings are formal (which may be because his native language is Spanish); the language is careful and considered. In fact, even when he finally homes in on the life-changing incident in Piura, he maintains an emotional distance from his narrative, *telling* the reader that he learns "something that constituted an emotional earthquake." His relation of what he learns is similarly styled to keep a distance between the narrator and his emotions— yes, it's amusing that a nine-year-old boy still believed babies were delivered by storks, but the deeper emotional chaos that the news seems to have created within Vargas Llosa is not shown on the page. The passage assumes the weight of a coming-of-age moment.

Vargas Llosa's formal, more intellectual style here does not, as one might initially believe, distance the reader from the narrative. Instead, it serves as a lasso, at first swinging in wide arcs, then circling in closer and closer to the heart of the matter, until we learn, a bit further on, that Vargas Llosa and his friends also spent many hours that summer spying on a green house that he learned years later was a brothel.

In the young boy's mind, the mysteries of childbirth become entangled with the green house, even though at that time he doesn't know they're both about sex. Even when, years later, he realizes they are, they lose none of their mystery but only fire his imagination more. In the end, Vargas Llosa has no choice but to turn his fascinations with these (and several other, seemingly unrelated) fictional seeds into his novel *The Green House*.

The Shadowy Personage Who Commits the Actual Writing

Whenever we (that is, Lynn and Lisa) talk about voice, we find ourselves citing Margaret Atwood. That's because, no matter what this queen of letters turns her pen to, her distinctive clever, witty, and, above all, arch style rings, and zings, true.

In *Negotiating with the Dead*, Atwood offers her own unique perspective on both writing and being a writer. Here, for example, she explores the duplicity that she insists is the root of a writer's art: "What is the relationship between the two entities we lump under one name, that of 'the writer'? . . . By *two*, I mean the person who exists when no writing is going forward—the one who walks the dog, eats bran for regularity, takes the car in to be washed, and so forth—and that other, more shadowy and altogether more equivocal personage who shares the same body, and who, when no one is looking, takes it over and uses it to commit the actual writing" (35).

What's particularly delightful about Atwood's style is its insistence on (to co-opt one of her word choices) "regularity." In talking about the writer when she's not writing, she might have used a phrase like "her everyday life" or "her daily chores." Instead, she chooses to name some specific activities—dog walking, breakfast eating, car washing—rendering the moment both more individual and more universal. It's this insistence on detailing the everyday, even within the most unusual of moments, that places an added stamp on Atwood's style. Whatever she says she does or doesn't do, we sense the hand of the writer at work.

"The Capsules of Safety, and Freedom"

By their very nature, poets bring a distinctive tang to their prose writing styles. In earlier chapters we've cited Mark Doty and Rachel Hadas, both of whom have written memoirs in addition to their many books of poetry, and in this chapter we refer to a memoir by poet Hilda Raz. Mary Oliver is another poet whose prose writings reflect her individual style.

While *Long Life* is a collection of essays and occasional writings, her inclusion of childhood remembrances even in these forms is a hallmark of Oliver's style. The following, for example, comes from an essay about Wordsworth:

> When I was a child, living in a small town surrounded by woods and a winding creek—woods more pastoral than truly wild—my great pleasure, and my secret, was to fashion for myself a number of little houses. They were huts, really, made of sticks and grass, maybe a small heap of fresh leaves inside. There was never a closure but always an open doorway, and I would sit just inside, looking out into the world. Such architectures were the capsules of safety, and freedom as well, open to the wind, made of grass and smelling like leaves and flowers. (22)

Poets are collectors of the details of everyday life who can later recount (and reorder) those details so that the moments they recollect are resurrected for the reader. Notice the accumulation of details here: the winding creek, the little huts "made of sticks and grass," "smelling like leaves and flowers."

At the same time, Oliver employs a conversational style, so that the reader feels as if he's listening to her speak rather than reading her words on the page. Markers of this style include the interjection—phrases set between dashes, like this one—and the colloquial tic, like "really" or the currently popular "well." This juxtaposition of poetic and narrative elements results in Oliver's unique voice and style, which are both elegiac and conversational. The result creates an intimacy between writer and reader, so that Oliver's voice, with its distinct details and easy style, whispers confidentially in the reader's ear.

CLAIMING YOUR VOICE

Like the voices of the masters we've cited above, your writing voice will be uniquely your own. The spotlight exercises earlier in this chapter are good first steps for honing that voice. Now we'd like to share a few more techniques from the Fiction Writer's Toolkit that will help you sharpen your voice still more.

You Are the Camera

The term *cinema verité* comes to us from French cinema, but the camera's-eye view to which it refers has become so common since the advent of handheld cameras that its originality when it was first pioneered is often overlooked. Imagine any scene in film where you, the viewer, are placed in the scene— often from the protagonist's point of view—and you will grasp the essence of cinema verité.

Point of view refers to the assumed eyes and ears of the "person" telling a story. In the case of memoir, this is almost always you.

As a writer, and especially as a writer of memoir, you can use cinema verité to striking effect. First, bear in mind that when you experienced what you are writing about, you *could not see yourself*. In other words, your memory allows you to become the camera. This gives you a unique perspective (in writing terms, *point of view*) of the goings-on. Because you're facing in a certain direction, you can't see everything—you can see the person next to you only in profile, what's behind you not at all. This means that, as the story's teller, you can *imagine* what you can't see, but you can't report it as if you actually saw it.

Vivid memoirs use the eye of the camera to marvelous effect. Here, for example, is Patricia Hampl, in *A Romantic Education*, remembering her grandmother offering her freshly baked rye bread: "The loaf was round, heavy and my grandmother held it to her bosom like a member of the family as she hacked off what was not a slice, but a hunk" (79). By giving us the child's point of view here, we, like the child Hampl, feel the grandmother's looming presence as well as the subliminal terror as she "hack[s] off . . . a hunk" of what she is holding so closely—the narrator can imagine being the object held just that way. Note the visceral language and the specificity of the image and how they convey emotion as well.

Our discussion of first, second, and third person earlier in this chapter also illustrates point of view as the "I" or "you" or "he/she" controls the amount of distance and limits the vision of the narrator.

SPOTLIGHT EXERCISE

Writing: Seeing visceral details through a camera's eye can help you convey their emotional weight. To try this yourself, pick a scene from your childhood where you are observing adults. Make notes to answer the following: Where are you? Where are they? What is going on? How do you feel about the physical presence of the adults in your view? Give a visceral detail for each that conveys your emotional response as well. To extend the exercise, write the scene in first person and then in third person. Compare the effect of each.

Using What You Don't Know

Once you really begin to think about the limits of point of view, you will inevitably need to consider how to incorporate what you don't know into your memoir. Memoirists use a variety of methods from the Fiction Writer's Toolkit for showing the reader things the memoirists couldn't possibly have known firsthand, including having another character tell the narrator about the event, photographs, letters (or e-mails)—or their imaginations.

Learning the truth about something later from someone else is not just a trope of the memoir but a fact of life. But what if you never do learn the truth? What if you must use the last tool we mentioned, your imagination, to complete your memoir? In Booker Award–winning author Penelope Lively's

Making It Up, which she calls an "antimemoir," the author chooses to dance between what she remembers and what she has imagined. As she notes in her preface, "Now, at the other end of life, storytelling is an ingrained habit. . . . This book is fiction. . . . My own life serves as the prompt; I have homed in upon the rocks, the rapids, the whirlpools, and written *the alternative stories*" (1–2, emphasis added).

Lively begins each section with an italicized event from her life and then uses something from that moment as the jumping-off point for an imagined narrative. In "Transatlantic," for example, she mentions a one-day encounter, when she's an undergraduate at Oxford, with an American professor whom she is assigned to show around. At the end of the day, the professor gives her his card and tells her, "My university has postgraduate programs that might appeal to you. Let me know if you're interested" (116). Lively never follows up on this offer. But in the fiction that follows the anecdote, she imagines an alternative life where she did.

Narrating imagined stories of what didn't happen can help you get closer to what did happen. You can even use them in your memoir, as Joan Didion does so eloquently in *The Year of Magical Thinking*. Didion continually circles back to the moment just before her husband, John, died, imagining that, via magical thinking, she might alter its outcome.

You can also use your imagination to write about something that happened to someone else that directly affects the story you are trying to tell but that, for one reason or another, you cannot ever know with complete certainty. What was going through your loved one's mind, for example, just before he or she died? How did the person you were arguing with feel about what you were saying? Did your mother have the same reaction you did when your father walked out the door for the last time? In chapter 7 we'll discuss walking the tightrope between authenticity and the self-truth of your story.

In such instances, for one reason or another, you can't ask the other person how she was feeling. But it's possible that now, as the remembering narrator, you can imagine how she might have felt, or, as Ellen Meloy puts it in *Eating Stone: Imagination and the Loss of the Wild*, "The human spirit . . . yearns for glimpses into the 'interiority' of a being that is different, not us, something not quite comprehensible, something that moves in its own complete universe. To bat-listen, to touch an otherworld with more than one sense, to reclaim daily the notion of layered miracles" (319).

To "bat-listen." Imagine the possibilities for your memoir.

We'd like to close this discussion with a reminder that while readers initially start a new book for the story, they stick around because they've come to care about the storyteller. Tell your story in a compelling voice, and you'll never lack for readers who care.

We hope these six chapters have helped you nurture the seeds of your memoir. In the next, and final, chapter we'll explore what happens when you finish your draft, including strategies for revision and rewriting, the trials and tribulations of being true to your story and its inhabitants, and how to bring your memoir out into the world.

7

Honoring the Memoir Process

Taking the Next Steps

All writing . . . is motivated . . . by a desire to make the risky trip to
the Underworld, and to bring something or someone back from
the dead.

—MARGARET ATWOOD, *Negotiating with the Dead:
A Writer on Writing*

There is nothing quite as satisfying as typing "The End" on a manuscript
you've spent months—or, more likely, years—writing. But that doesn't mean
you're finished. To us, completing the first draft means that the fun can begin:
now we can dig down and mine the ore of what we really want to say.

"The discoveries we make during revision are a vital part of the writing
process," Sue William Silverman notes in *Fearless Confessions* (24). The word
"discoveries" is key here. What a writer learns about the past in the process of
revision and rewriting can hold the key to what makes a particular memoir
shine. As Silverman puts it, "It's only through writing about events after they
happen—as we craft our memoirs—that we come to understand what they
mean" (45).

RE-VISIONING YOUR MANUSCRIPT

While almost every writing teacher you encounter will sing the praises of
revision and rewriting, every writer will ultimately need to find his or her
own path through what often feels like a thicket. For an example very close to
the page, each one of us—Lynn and Lisa—has a distinctly different approach
to both writing and revision. What this amounts to, in the end, is that we're
simply hiking the same terrain wearing different shoes. We decided it would
be most helpful to you if we consolidated our different methods into a menu
of options you can try yourself.

Read It Aloud

Lynn, a performer and director as well as a writer, learned early on how the act of writing lives in the body as well as incubates in the mind. When a passage proves difficult, reading it aloud often provides an answer or at least inspiration. Poets in particular extol the virtues of using the audible voice when writing. The first stories, after all, were shared in community and passed down from person to person. Albert Lord's elemental book *The Singer of Tales* is an excellent resource for learning about early oral culture.

Performing your chapters aloud, whether to yourself, to friends, or to writing group members, lets you hone your voice and develop your ear. Awkwardness is easy to hear when you read aloud. Use this technique to explore the pace and rhythms of your language and voice, too. It's particularly good for making sure scenes are vital: elements like rising and falling action, tempo, and balance of internal with external action become heightened.

At the same time, putting your work out there in acoustic space makes it real: the voice takes on timbre and tone and changes the quality of the room, the body and mind come together, and words become palpable. As Donald Hall notes in his 1985 essay, "Bring Back the Out-Loud Culture," "If when we read silently we do not hear a text, [then] we slide past words passively, without making decisions, without knowing or caring about [the words' tone]. . . . In the old Out-Loud Culture, print was always potential speech; even silent readers, too shy to read aloud, inwardly heard the sound of words."

The act of writing itself employs the hand, the eye, and the brain. But when we read aloud, the whole dimension of the physical opens up. One of Lynn's favorite ways to begin a revision, whether her own or a student's, involves having another person read the writer's words so that the writer can sit back and hear them outside of himself. Nothing improves the nuances of dialogue more than reading aloud. Spoken dialogue has to pass the "authenticity" test—a wrong word, an awkward phrasing, a broken flow are all easily revealed. Some writers write standing up in order to further heighten the physicality of writing. Many writers choose to write in longhand rather than on the computer for this reason. However you choose to do it, the more aspects of yourself you involve in your creation, the more deeply you claim your authorship.

Put It Away

In Lisa's book about writing fiction, *The Mind of Your Story*, she emphasizes the importance of printing out a copy of your manuscript as soon as you type

"The End" and then *putting it away.* Lisa has found that the creation of a physical document, as opposed to a file on her computer, one that she puts in a three-ring binder that joins its companions on a bookshelf, pulls the manuscript off her left brain's front burner so that she can move on to other projects.

While Lisa prefers to let manuscripts sit for six months or even longer, this isn't always possible when a project (like this one) has a deadline. So when she drafts her monthly column for Authorlink.com, for example, she prints it out and sets it aside overnight, then edits it and prints out a new copy, doing this for several days until she's satisfied with the result.

Not everyone needs a hard copy, of course, but Lisa has found that a hard copy's physical presence provides a powerful incentive to move on to another project. Equally important to her is longhand editing when she returns to the manuscript after its closet time. Whether you choose to edit in longhand or on the screen is ultimately your choice.

Take It Out

A comfortable chair, a colored pen, sticky tabs—these are Lisa's primary tools for revision and rewriting. The colored pen makes her edits stand out from the black print (she prefers blue ink, but any color will do); the sticky tabs mark thematic issues she wants to make certain are carried through, plot points that need to be brought to conclusion, and other narrative threads that she doesn't want to forget when she finishes her read-through.

While she's looking at these holistic issues, at the same time Lisa is line editing—adding and subtracting or changing words, moving or deleting phrases and sentences, writing "awk" (for "awkward") in the margin so she can address passages for clarity when she types in her edits, getting rid of word repetitions, and tightening up her prose to the point where she won't be embarrassed to see her name above it.

Lynn prefers to do her editing on her computer. Each time we've edited a chapter in this book, Lynn has typed her changes using Microsoft Word's Track Changes feature, while Lisa has first scribbled all over a hard copy and then entered them. You may well find a middle ground when you begin your own revision. Each of us employs different strategies to visualize and apprehend the component parts—and the totality—of the manuscript. The point is that you should play with different approaches until you find what works best for you.

Both of us, however, have found that, because we have put our manuscripts away for a period of time, a marvelous thing has happened: we can revisit them without being married to anything we've written. We come back to our work with an editorial rather than an authorial eye and so are able to cut away the most gorgeous phrases for the greater good of the larger piece. The editorial eye sees the holistic picture, not just the priceless prose of one section. By all means keep your priceless prose in a separate "outtakes" file, because such tidbits often become the seeds of future works.

In *On the Teaching of Creative Writing*, Wallace Stegner refers to "the laboratory of pen, paper, and wastebasket" (59). We can't stress enough how much the latter is the writer's friend. Don't be afraid to throw things out. If something "feels" wrong, it probably is. If a phrase hits the ear with a false note, pay attention. Read the paragraph aloud without the offending portion to determine if it's needed. Or, if something's clearly missing, scribble it in the margin. If you're dealing with a longer scene, open a new file in your computer and type it out. As this, too, will be edited later, there's no need to get it just so this first time. Just get it on the page, if it needs to be there. Throwing things out does not mean permanently deleting them. We believe words can be recycled.

An Editorial Checklist

Revising your work involves reexamining both the big picture and the smaller details. The idea of fixing everything that seems problematic can be daunting, especially if you're new to the process. We suggest you approach revision in sections rather than attempting to tackle everything at once.

We usually begin with big-picture aspects of structure and plot: Do the elements work together and in a sequence that leads the reader where we want her to go? A key issue here is intentionality: What do you hope the reader will feel or think by the end of the book?

Revision is a process that allows you to see your work in a new way. We've organized the following as a series of questions prompting you to bring a fresh vision to your story. By taking you through this revision series with the major themes of each chapter, we're aiming to allow you to make the best use of the spotlight writing exercises throughout the book.

The Occasion of the Telling

These questions encourage you to distill the catalyst for your story, giving the reader a context for all that follows. Your occasion of the telling grounds both you, the writer, and your reader. It introduces the story and why it's important and gives the reader a reason to keep going. Keynotes for the occasion of the telling are *immediacy* and *consequence*.

1. Is the *opening* effective?
2. *What* does the narrator *want*?
3. Why does this memoir begin *now*?

The Two Yous

The two yous establish the collaboration of the experiencing narrator in the past and the remembering narrator in the present. While both of these selves coexist, thinking of them as distinct brings to the forefront the transformation the speaker undergoes through the journey of the story. The two yous directly proceed from the occasion of the telling and bind the story in time and space.

1. Does the story move back and forth clearly in *time*?
2. Does the remembering narrator have a *place to stand*?
3. Is the experiencing narrator anchored in time?
4. Does the memoir's structure accommodate the *movement between the two yous*?

Building a Narrative

Plot and structure are the basis of your story. Here you'll look at what the story is about (plot) and the mode of its telling (structure). As we explored in chapters 3 and 4, not only does action have an arc, but it rises and falls, suggesting more than one way your story can unfold for the reader. As you revise, you'll take a fresh look at what incites your story, how the scenes work to carry it forward, and the structural umbrella for the story. This checklist is extensive, because plot and structure touch every aspect of your memoir.

1. What is the *basic idea* of the story?
2. What is the *chief question* of the story? (The occasion of the telling is most useful here.)
3. How will the story be *arranged* (chronologically, circularly, etc.)?
4. *Who* wants *what*?
5. Who or what *stands in the way* of this aim?
6. What *plan* does the protagonist make toward reaching his or her goal?
7. What *opposes* him or her?
8. What are the *qualities* of the conflict? Are they largely internal or external?
9. How is the action *started*?

10. Is the conflict established *early* in the story?

11. With which characters do you want the reader to *sympathize*?

12. What's at stake?

Arranging the Scenes

Scenes are the building blocks of your narrative, each beginning with a catalyst and then rising in either internal or external action that keeps the reader
actively engaged in the story. Reordering and rearranging scenes can be one
of the most rewarding aspects of the revision process, so pay attention to
where in your narrative each scene belongs as well as how well it works. Don't
be afraid to pick up sections as well as paragraphs or entire scenes and move
them to another place. Just be sure to save your original work with a new file
name (and date) before you begin your revision. Another way to approach
this process is to construct a visual scene map or a brainstorming diagram.

1. Does the scene *belong*?

2. Does it belong *where it is*?

3. Is it *awkward*?

4. Is it there for the *reader* or for the *writer*?

5. Are there passages that need *expansion*?

6. How can they be *enhanced*?

7. Does the story *move forward*?

8. Does it *mount in tension*?

9. Is *each scene functional*?

10. Does the climax *dramatize/complete* my intention for the story?

Painting the Picture

Distinctive language and details are the workhorses of good writing and can
reveal character as well as keep your story moving forward. Once you've finished your first draft, patterns of imagery and metaphor will reveal themselves and can be tightened to your narrative's advantage. You'll also want to
check your details for historical accuracy and make sure your setting is as
vivid as possible. This is a good moment to make sure that your metaphors
are true to your milieu and that you have double-checked for anachronisms.
The best settings are as distinctive as vivid characters.

1. Are my *characters* true to themselves?

2. Is my *dialogue* (and attribution) accurate?

3. Is the *environment/place* palpable to the reader?

4. Do the details take on an aspect of *character*?

Your Story, Your Voice

Discovering your voice is one of the most exciting revelations of writing your story. But because your writing voice is different from your speaking voice, you will want to revise with an ear toward getting rid of the overly casual and often circuitous ways we tend to speak. Use the questions below to hone your writing voice and to make it more clearly your own. This is a place where reading aloud is crucial.

1. If this were not your memoir, how would you describe *the voice that you hear*?

2. Do I *say the same thing twice* in different ways?

3. Are there places that need *tightening*?

4. Does this voice *sound true* to the two yous in this memoir?

5. Do the *descriptions* enhance your narrative?

Honoring the Memoir Process

Once you've attended to all of the matters above, take a hard look at your memoir as a whole, considering these bigger questions as you do so.

1. Do the parts fit together as *a whole*?

2. Is there anything *extraneous*?

3. Does the ending seem *inevitable*?

4. Am I honoring the *integrity* of my story?

5. Do I allow family members and friends to have *their own version of events*?

6. Can I withstand the *public scrutiny* of my story?

While there are other issues that can arise in a manuscript, we've found that authors who can answer each of these questions succinctly are well on their way to a polished product.

OTHER PEOPLE, OTHER ROOMS

Nearly every writer of memoir struggles with the dilemma of public versus private in exposing a memoir to the larger world. Do we have the right to tell our stories, knowing that other people will be affected by what we reveal, particularly family members, close friends, and spouses? In the pages of this book we've cited numerous authors, many of whom discuss the process itself and, in particular, the importance of claiming your story. As Laura Furman says in her memoir, *Ordinary Paradise*, "Writing is the best way I know to remember us all" (6).

The sharing of these life events may cause discomfort to others to whom you are close, but we write about particular times in our lives because we must. In the same way that our voices must be heard, we must write our stories, because for those of us who choose to do so, it is the only way to integrate those events and make sense of them enough to move forward in our lives.

Claiming Responsibility for Your Story

In *Searching for Mercy Street*, Linda Gray Sexton explores in detail how she was compelled to write about her fraught relationship with her mother, the poet Anne Sexton. Almost ten years after her mother's death, Linda Gray Sexton discovered that her writing was suffering (this after publishing four novels): "This time the more I had tried to hide behind the wall of my fiction, the less I was able to produce. . . . Perhaps what I needed to do was to write about the issue directly. No disguises this time around. No more running away" (300).

Dani Shapiro records a similar difficulty that caused her to begin her memoir *Slow Motion*: "I felt stuck in my fiction. . . . My three novels all revolved around a central calamity. I felt like my own autobiographical material was controlling me. It was clear that I needed to wrestle my past to the ground. I needed to pin it in time, to capture it as if it were a wild animal that I could domesticate—or at least put behind bars" (interview reprinted in *Slow Motion*, back matter, p. 10).

Similarly, in his essay "Lifting the Veil," Henry Louis Gates Jr. writes that when he wrote his memoir *Colored People*, he had to tell family and racial secrets, even though many people approached him and said, "Did you fear that this was a risk?" Gates answers: "The answer is yes. But I wasn't any more honest about our culture or about my mother's family than I was about myself. That was important to me. I took myself as the bottom line. I think mine is the first generation of black people in America who can afford to be this open" (109).

Like Gates, many writers feel that their greatest role as artists is to lift the veil and reveal the pain of their lives, which often centers on their race, class, or sexuality. As Toni Morrison says in "The Site of Memory," "My job becomes how to rip that veil drawn over 'proceedings too terrible to relate.' The exercise is also critical for any person who is black, or who belongs to any marginalized category, for, historically, we were seldom invited to participate in the discourse even when we were its topic" (191). Part of telling the truth of our lives is digging deep into its challenges. We must write where the energy is.

The Ethics of Guilt

Some writers have found that they can assuage the guilt or shame of revealing the difficulties or challenges in their lives through the effects of their stories on readers. Others take courage and find validation when they read a story that underscores their life experience. When we spoke in chapter 1 of the power of witnessing, we weren't suggesting that the writer has an ethical obligation to share the hard journeys but rather that capturing the pain of the human experience and bringing it to light for others is right and ethical for many writers.

Ian Frazier addresses the guilt that many encounter as they reveal what not only others but often they themselves feel should be kept secret. In "Looking for My Family," he notes: "There's no escaping that—guilt is the headwind that you sail into. It's incredibly strong" (180). Frazier insists that you absolutely can combat this guilt, whether by giving your money to charity or through some other means. In addition, he suggests asking permission of those who are in your story. "Guilt is a form of narcissism," he says (ibid.).

Each writer has to put his or her own demons to rest on this issue. There isn't a template for how to handle the thorny issues of bringing personal stories into the public realm. Fortunately, many have written about the guilt of revealing family stories as well as about the secrets of their own lives and have lived through the struggle to find that the end result—the connection with others through their choice to reveal the truth—is worth the challenges. Henry Louis Gates Jr. gives us these words of advice: "Be prepared for the revelation of things you don't even dream are going to come up" (108).

Writing, any kind of writing, is risky. Your job is to take the risk.

WHAT'S NEXT?

Once you have a draft of your memoir that you've either revised to your satisfaction or that you find you can't revise any further at present, your next step is to seek feedback. When you've brought your manuscript along as far as you can, it can be because either you feel you've run out of ideas, your momentum is flagging, or you feel plain stuck. While you may know you want or need to change the structure, adjust the plot, improve the details, or deal with other issues, you're just not sure how to accomplish this.

Rest assured that this "out of gas" state of mind comes to all writers at one time or another and that it signals the need for other people's opinions. That's right: your story now requires an audience to develop further. If you're already a member of a critique group or a writing support group, now is the time to ask the group to read your work and offer comments. If you don't have a group like this, you may be able to start one with writers with a similar level of commitment, find one online, take a writing class, or venture to one of the many writing conferences held across the country throughout the year.

A strange but frequently experienced paradox of sharing your work is that, while you can easily picture yourself at a book signing or talking to Oprah about your work, the idea of sharing it with people you know can be scary. We feel exposed when we open our work to criticism and feedback. Like stage fright, this feeling never goes away entirely, but we increasingly appreciate that the benefits—the validation we receive and the steady improvement of our writing—outweigh our discomfort.

Some writers use family members or friends as sounding boards, especially when they wish to get reactions from others who know part of the story they're telling. These readers will have a familiarity with the cultural setting of the memoir and therefore can be asked about the authenticity of the memoir's world. For others, this group of people closest to the work is one to be avoided: sometimes when people have something at stake (their truth versus yours, perhaps), they cannot overcome their subjective investment in the story. To them, it's *their* story too, and this can create a conflict. At the same time, those closest to you may be unwilling or unable to offer the critical response you need at this juncture. Praise is marvelous, but when we're stuck, we need to know what's wrong and how we might fix it. At some point, each memoir writer must approach the issue of involving intimate others in his own way.

As we discussed earlier in this chapter, you have an ethical responsibility toward your own story both to be as accurate as you can and to find its essential truth through the process of writing it down. It's natural to want to spare the feelings of others, especially those closest to us, and yet that isn't always possible, not if consideration of others hampers our realization of the story we're telling. As Alice Kaplan notes in "Lady of the Lake," "*Writing about yourself is a high-wire balancing act between revelation and a need to set bounds, to respect your own need for privacy and the right to privacy of others"* (99, emphasis in the original).

For all these reasons, you will want to find others with whom to share your work who respect your right to tell your story, treat the writing with the respect and care it deserves, and genuinely share your desire to make the end result as good as it can be. This last, enhancing the writing and execution of the story as much as possible, is paramount in the feedback process.

SPOTLIGHT EXERCISE

Writing: Who are the voices in your head? Are they encouraging you? If so, what are they saying? Write down their words of encouragement. Or, conversely, are they trying to stop you from telling your story? If that's the case, write down who these voices are and the roadblocks they're putting in your way. By identifying how others feel about your story, you honor *their* place in *your* story. Either way, whether the voices in your head are cheering you on or creating self-doubt, you must assert your right to speak and claim your story.

Bringing Your Story into Public Space

Writing groups or a writing coach or teacher can give you a detailed critique that addresses specific issues in your draft. Other avenues of voicing your story in public space include:

1. *Open mics*: Most communities have places where writers can read their works to small audiences with question-and-answer sessions or talkbacks afterward. The Q&A, especially if moderated by a friend or colleague, allows your audience to respond to specific aspects of the memoir.
2. *Talks to specific groups*: Preparing a chapter or a specific section of a memoir as a talk to a community, social, or church group is another way to air the material and have the audience weigh in. Most memoirs deal with challenging life situations. Groups exist to advise and provide support for family members with illnesses, those dealing with a death in their family, or spousal issues. Talks like these are an excellent way to identify the sections of the manuscript that resonate with others. They are also a great way to build the future audience for purchasing your book once it has been published.

3. *Writing or artist conferences*: Take the memoir or sections of it to writing retreats, summer conferences, or local writing organization meetings where it can benefit from the workshop process. At the very least this kind of forum imbues your manuscript with credibility. Once out in the world, the manuscript touches others and is shaped in return.

4. *Classes or critique groups*: Writing or revising chunks of your manuscript in a creative writing class or a generative writing or critique group allows you to polish your memoir in a supportive environment. Classes can provide critical tools for honing your work. In a generative or critique writing environment, as others grow familiar with your writing and your story, the group can help you identify any remaining problem areas as well as provide emotional support and community.

Your Story, Your Book

Walking the line between others' demands and your own need for confession and closure will almost certainly require some tough choices. But, in the end, your memoir is *your* recording of *your* story. The toughest question as you begin is deciding whether it's more important for you to achieve catharsis by sharing your story or to acquiesce to the wishes of those who may be hurt or offended by what you must write. Once you're convinced of the necessity and importance of writing your story, no matter what others think, you're well on your way.

In this book we've endeavored to show you that writing a successful memoir is far more than simply writing down what you remember. Using the Fiction Writer's Toolkit, you can write a story that can make a difference to others, whether they're negotiating a similar rite of passage, wishing to learn about lives different from their own, or seeking marvelous stories.

Using the tools we've provided, you're now ready to turn your experience into a story that will resonate with others and to begin a process that will teach you much about yourself. We look forward to reading your work!

Spotlight Exercises by Chapter

CHAPTER 1. THE OCCASION OF THE TELLING

Writing: Think about stories that have resonated throughout your life. First, choose an often-told family story: jot down a description of the central character and how you came to hear about the story. Why do you think this story was handed down in your family? What did it illustrate? Second, note a story you've read, whether fiction or memoir, young adult or fable. How does the story begin? What event or thought causes the hero to make a break with the past or embark on a new path?

This exercise illustrates how the classic structure resonates in the stories we've heard all our lives.

Writing: Using the notes you made in the spotlight exercise about family stories earlier in this chapter, take one story you remember and play with its organization in time. Try to come up with three versions of how it could be told. For example, if the story were told by an older sibling, how might it begin? How might the speaker go from now to then and back? Another example is noting how the story's time sense would change if three or four members of the family chimed in to tell the story. Each might start events in a different place and give the listener a different context.

Reading: Compare the occasion of the telling in two of the memoirs from the works cited or from books of your choice. Are you committed to read further after reading the writer's occasion? Why or why not?

Writing: List five events in your life that are significant. Maybe they involve specific people or a move from one place to another. Maybe they spotlight other transitions, or possibly they are key turning points that haunt you. Don't think too much; just write them down.

Taking each of the five events from the previous paragraph, imagine a photograph that captures some essence of the event. Write down a detailed description of what is in that photograph. What is in the foreground? What is in the background? What (or who) is not in the photograph, even though you know that person or thing should be a part of it? Who might have taken the photograph, if it were real?

Now choose one of the images from the above paragraph and make it move. Begin to construct a scene around that moving photograph. What happens because of what event or person? Again, don't think too much; just try to get down this key moment in as much detail as you can.

Chapter 2. The Two Yous

Writing: "A memoirist gazes at a canvas that's already swirling with color," Sue William Silverman writes in *Fearless Confessions*. "Where a fiction writer crafts images onto that blank canvas, the memoirist decides what to remove from it" (31).

Consider the canvas of a scene from your past you'd like to re-create on paper as if it were a still life. Now take a further step back and consider yourself considering that scene. Observe the observer you. What does she see now that she didn't see then? What does she think about what she's observing? Without judging either of the two yous, make some notes about the remembering you studying the experiencing you.

Reading: Choose a passage from a memoir you admire (you may wish to choose one we've mentioned in this chapter) where you notice the narrator shifting between the two yous. What perspective(s) does this movement in time provide toward your understanding the protagonist more deeply? Are there gaps between the narrator's assessment of the events in this passage and what you perceive as a reader? Often the reader makes connections that the writer may not consciously have intended. It's through these connections that author and reader witness each other and that the reader gains new understanding.

Reading: During the Middle Ages, alchemists sought to turn lesser elements into gold. While their experiments couldn't succeed, as a writer you possess the tools to, as we note above, "turn raw emotion into art." The first of these tools, of course, is the memories themselves. But negotiating this territory requires a willingness to mine, and then refine, your work.

Find a passage in a memoir you've read where the author has clearly gone somewhere difficult. How does he use his two yous to negotiate this territory? What would be missing if the remembering narrator weren't there? Employing a remembering narrator to witness his difficult return can be a key to negotiating it.

Writing: In conversation, we seldom pay attention to the way we use language. There may be moments when we choose our words more carefully—when we need to get a point across, or when we're disagreeing with someone about whom we care deeply—but most of us use our own particular everyday diction to express what we wish to share with others verbally.

How we express ourselves in writing, however, involves a more elevated diction or, put another way, a selection and reordering of words and phrases to convey meaning on the page. When we add the two yous to this equation, it becomes all the more challenging a prospect.

For this exercise, select a moment from your past that you hope to include in your memoir. First, write the scene as you remember it, using words and the writing skill you possess now, as a remembering narrator.

When you've finished this scene, put it away. Now write the same scene as if you were once again that younger you. Nothing you've learned since that moment can enter into this writing—not words, not experience, not hindsight. Try to use active verbs that bring to life the emotions you were experiencing then, and don't forget to include more than just visual senses—add sounds, scents, tastes, feelings.

After finishing the second scene, read the two versions. Chances are, there will be parts of each of them that will work very well for your memoir. If you want to take this exercise one step further, try moving back and forth between these two yous to interweave these two renditions into one scene containing both your voices.

Writing: Choosing a memory from an exercise in chapter 1 or another memory that occurs to you right now, write a few paragraphs establishing the you who is remembering now, looking back on yourself in the past. Move back and forth between what you recall and how you view the incident/experience/action now. The insights you are able to bring to bear on the past as you do this illustrate the power of the remembering self and your ability to frame your experience with a depth the experiencing self cannot access.

Reading: Now read what you have written and answer the following questions: What are several possibilities for where to stand in recounting this particular memory? Is there one place that feels compelling to you? Why?

CHAPTER 3. BUILDING A NARRATIVE

Writing: Let's pause for a moment to consider how you might apply a catalyst to your own memoir. Take some time now to select one of the occasions of the telling you recorded at the end of chapter 1. Next, write down one or more catalysts that could trigger a specific first scene in your memoir. Don't censor; write down whatever first comes to you. While these events may not begin your memoir, they may very well be clues to other chapters or significant scenes in the narrative.

Writing: Because we experience time sequentially, a chronological structure is a good one to try out first. Beginning with the catalyst that you noted earlier in this chapter, list in chronological order what will happen in your memoir.

Reading and writing: The best circularly structured memoirs work because they have a narrative anchor—a touchstone that the remembering narrator (and by association the reader) returns to throughout the story. For an anchor to work, it must be powerful enough to support a circular narrative, have larger metaphoric resonance, and have the associative strength to engage your reader. Consider the catalyst you noted at the beginning of this chapter. Is there a touchstone within in? It may not be obvious at first look. Touchstones can be anything from a spot on a wall to the sound of thunder. List some possible touchstones for your own memoir, and if one provides some immediate resonance for you, keep going and see where it takes you. See if you can successfully circle back to it and if it retains its sensuous aura when you do.

Writing: Associating memories with a place or a time period allows us to begin to develop a sense of interlocking events, in turn leading us to plot. Draw a time line on a piece of paper and begin to insert key places and occurrences. Do some notations connect to others or associate with other times in your life? Alternatively, if you're a spatial person, set up physical markers in a room that represent key events. As you move from one marker to another, see if you can come up with a gesture that expresses it. Do you walk more quickly or slowly to certain events? That body response helps you create rhythm in your narrative and gives you clues about where you'd like to augment the details.

Writing: Imagine your story as a collection of objects. List the objects, then describe the textures and qualities of these objects in a notebook. Alternatively, think of a key event in your life and try to envision it as a series of photographs. What is the quality of the light in the images? What is the overall mood or tone of the pictures? The sensory details you'll record in this exercise will help you to create strong physical/textural details in your story.

Reading and writing: Joan Weimer was already researching the life of Constance Fenimore Woolson when her back problems began, but using Woolson's life as a vehicle for mirroring Weimer's own difficulties occurred to her only over time. Nonetheless, we are drawn to certain historical characters because something about their lives resonates for us. The two of us, for example, return again and again to the life and work of Katherine Anne Porter, a writer born in challenging circumstances who transformed herself into a woman of letters, as we make sense of our own lives as writers.

Are there people from the past whose lives fascinate you? They don't necessarily need to be public figures—our own ancestors can provide keys to current dilemmas in our own lives. Take a moment to make a list of historical people by whom you're intrigued. If one seems to provide particular resonance, make a note of that, too, and, if you wish, write a few paragraphs to see where that person takes you.

Reading and writing: Often, when we say "place," we think of larger places—houses, cities, office buildings, and the like. But "place" encompasses smaller places, too—your childhood room, for example, or the restaurant where you meet friends each week.

Do the places in your life organize themselves into some cohesive theme, like Mars's places of worship or Gilbert's three countries that begin with the letter *I*? Are there commonalities among the places you've lived, the rooms where you've spent a lot of time, or are there patterns to your movement to or away from them? Make a list of places, large or small, that have figured in your life. Then draw some lines between them, not limiting yourself to obvious, immediate connections like chronology but instead thinking associatively. Write the association that precipitated the connection on the line itself. (Use a different color, if you like.) Play with these places, trying to imagine a memoir that uses them as its structure.

Writing: A good place to begin your consideration of what structure might work for you is with an informal list of what you hope your audience will take away from your memoir. Mention ideas as well as feelings. For example, do you hope that a story about a dear friend's illness will prompt the reader to discover the gifts as well as the tolls of the illness? This list will point you not only toward events you'll want to include but also, more importantly, toward the aspects of the self you wish to reveal in this project.

Reading: Which of the structures presented in this chapter allow you, given your subject matter and/or the occasion of the telling, the most possibilities for discovery?

Writing: Choose one structure and sketch out what it might allow you to reveal. Are there disadvantages to this structure that you can see? Is it restrictive in any way? How?

Reading and writing: Write down the qualities you enjoy most in a narrative. Choose one of the memoirs discussed in this chapter that has some of those qualities. How does its structure contribute to your reading enjoyment?

Chapter 4. Arranging the Scenes

Writing: Think for a moment of the spotlit moments you recorded in chapter 1. The fact that these memories remain with you suggests that they are catalysts, fragments from which individual scenes might unspool. Even if you can't recall what happened after the key image, writing it down will often unstop the memories you think you've lost.

So, without thinking about it, pick one of those moments now. Consider what has brought you, its protagonist, to this moment. Is there someone else in the picture? Who wants what? Make some notes as answers come to you. By the end of this chapter you'll have used this spotlit moment to create a complete scene. Working on one scene at a time can keep you from being overwhelmed by the idea of writing your whole story.

At the same time, be aware, as Patricia Hampl points out in *I Could Tell You Stories*, that your initial creation of this scene may contain some elements that don't belong there. This isn't a problem; always bear in mind that your first attempt at recording a spotlit moment is a draft—a starting point for digging deeper. As soon as we begin to write about the past our memories toss in all sorts of subliminal detritus. One of the great joys of writing memoir is that we'll get to sort this detritus into a larger truth, discarding what isn't essential and expanding upon what is. It's important at this generative stage not to censor or edit but simply to let the story emerge.

Writing: Consider the spotlit moment you noted above. There you are at an earlier moment in your life, captured in a still photograph in your mind's eye. Now, using what you wanted in that moment, put that photograph in motion. You want ——. But —— stands in your way.

Maybe you're sitting on a swing and want to keep swinging higher and higher, but it's getting dark, and you have to be home before dark. Conflict.

Maybe you've been forbidden to see the person who has just called you, but you want to see them. Conflict.

Maybe you're scowling at someone outside the frame. Why? Conflict.

Maybe there's a war on, and you must get out of the place you are in. Conflict.

Record any sensory images of that conflict: qualities of light, expression, gesture.

Reading: Consider the catalyst you recorded earlier in this chapter. What did the you in that moment want, and what stood in your way? What happens when you put that moment into motion? Does dialogue spring forth, an exchange where you express your desire and someone else says no? Or are you sitting in your childhood room, *imagining* what might happen if you attempt to fulfill your desire? Or does this scene occur *after* your desire was thwarted? In the latter two instances, your scene will immediately move into a moment outside the story's chronological time frame to deepen the opposition—in the first case into an imagined future, in the latter into the past. We'll consider the use of flashbacks, and "flashforwards," in chapter 5.

Reading and writing: Not all scenes have reversals, but we've found that when writers employ them, readers are "hooked" all the more. In a sense, the workings of plot and scene weave the reader into the action. Consider the scene you've been working on through the exercises in this chapter. Does something unexpected happen that surprises either the experiencing you or the remembering you? Bear in mind, too, that seemingly unrelated external occurrences can affect a narrator: something as simple as a bluebird's trill might cause someone to realize that life is worth living after all, or a neighbor's dog's incessant barking might drive her in the opposite direction.

The experiencing narrator can effect a reversal as well: the you in the past might be purposefully acting on his desire when he suddenly remembers (and remembering is an internal action) something that causes him to reassess his actions or the behavior of those around him.

Take a few moments here to record a few possible reversals for the scene you're working on. Remember, this is only a draft, a time to explore possibilities. You'll have as much time as you need to revisit it again and again.

Reading and writing: The scene you've been working on in this chapter has been moving toward its own turning point. The drama in a scene's epiphany does not have to be concussive. In fact, the quietest shifts can have far more emotional impact than the loudest explosions. People lean in closer to hear whispers, and readers who must imagine themselves into a scene are more intimately connected to it than those who have been forced in.

This is not to say that your scene won't have a literal explosion at its climax. But as the one who first experienced it and who now is reenvisioning it, you are the one who knows—and records—when the desire and opposition set in motion by your catalyst crescendo to their breaking point.

One of the beauties of the two yous is that there is more than one possible epiphany to your scene. You might apply knowledge you've gained only years after the fact (a letter you don't know about until someone else's death, for example). Even if an external event sends the scene in its moment in a new direction (that trilling bluebird, say), that event might send the experiencing you back to the first time you experienced it and how it made you feel. Recall the young Annie Dillard we referenced in chapter 3, recording her child-self acknowledged by the passing woman who notes Annie's exuberance.

Rather than demand only one climax for your scene during this first draft, we suggest that you instead list as many possibilities as you can, considering how the scene's present, past, and future might affect it. Don't worry about structure, spelling, or grammar—don't even try for complete sentences at this point unless they come naturally. Just note as many possible climaxes as you can.

Writing: Your own scene's denouement will arise out of the architecture you've built of rising, falling, and climactic action. Take a moment now to record the moment *after* each of the epiphanies you imagined for your scene in the previous section. The experiencing you might move forward—or step back. The remembering you might comment, imagine, or conjecture. The important thing is to provide the reader with some sense that the narrator acknowledges what has happened in the scene while at the same time his or her larger narrative arc continues to move forward.

Writing: Go back now to your scene's catalyst—the shimmering image with which you began. What did you see, hear, smell, taste, and feel when you first reimagined that moment? Take time to list words and sensory details that you can later use to re-create that image for readers. It's unlikely you'll use them all, so don't worry about that at this point. Even if you don't use them, the excavation you do will reveal itself in a more layered narrative, as we mentioned in the discussion of scaffolding in chapter 3. Simply list things like "blue sky," "smell of coffee," "the feel of the old wood banister" that you can later flesh out, as Dillard has.

Writing: Even if the scene you've been working with in this chapter is not external, it nonetheless occurs in some physical space that requires external delineation, and even if it's a quiet space, it nonetheless can be described by active verbs. Your childhood bedroom, for example, might "calm" or "frighten." A coffee shop might "clatter" or "chatter." Make a list of strong verbs that *show* the external action of your scene. As always, you'll return to this later, so don't worry about getting things perfect this first time out.

Writing: The examples we've provided of emblematic moments are complex ones, but such moments can be deceptively simple as well. We've noticed that what we call "first-date" stories—the details about ourselves we choose to share when we first meet someone—often contain such moments.

What are your first-date stories? Perhaps you always tell about the time you ran out of gas in the middle of nowhere, or, conversely, how you were the one who figured out how to get a stalled elevator full of people in motion again. Each of these stories reveals something you believe to be emblematic about you—whether or not they truly are. So begin this exercise by writing down your go-to first-date story. Try to write it as you tell it, keeping its dramatic structure to the form you've mastered over the years.

In *The Situation and the Story*, Vivian Gornick notes that memoir requires that the narrator have a stance that sustains his or her story. Once you've recorded your first-date story, put it away for a day or two. Then reread it with an eye toward the stance that you, its narrator, have taken regarding the you in the story. Do you use this story to illustrate what a contrary person you once were? Or to show that you've always been a take-charge sort?

Emblematic moments are keys into the two yous. Pay attention to them, and they'll help you map potential paths for your story.

Reading: Pick a scene from a memoir and explore why it does or doesn't work as a scene. Observe the balance of internal and external action. How does the scene engage the reader?

Writing: Create a dynamic scene in your memoir from anywhere in the story. By dynamic we mean a scene that has a dramatic arc, uses sensory details and a specific moment in time/space to reveal character or further the action, or creates a parallel image/event to reinforce a main theme or throughline. Be as specific as you can to *show* the action.

CHAPTER 5. PAINTING THE PICTURE

Reading: Choose a scene from a memoir and identify the kind and quality of metaphoric language used as the protagonist remembers the past or paints a picture for the reader of a specific time or place. What are some specific ways the writer involves you in the sensory images of the scene by using metaphor or symbol? Note any techniques of using figurative language you find compelling that you might use in your story.

Writing: Take one of the scenes you were working on in the exercises in chapter 4, or one of your possible entry points for the occasion of the telling in chapter 1, and experiment with creating metaphors for the action or characters. Use the list below to help you create comparisons that enhance the experiential qualities of your writing. In each case, use figurative writing to connote a sensuous comparison for a feeling, movement, or description.

Animal characteristics: We often compare the qualities or movements of animals to human behavior. Foxes, for example, are thought of as clever, magpies as thieves. Play with the animal characteristics your narrator and characters already possess and see what comes of it.

Color: Many people experience emotional states as colors, and even for those who don't, color imparts mood and tone. What does blue mean to you? Red? Yellow? Are your associations visual? Emotional? Physical? Do you hear certain things when you see certain colors? Try assigning each character in your memoir a color. What color are you?

Texture: Not only have sewing and weaving metaphors come to signify layers and levels of storytelling, but how something feels or looks in three dimensions grabs our attention. How does that blanket, that beach, that cold doorknob *feel*? Show it on the page.

Sound: Auditory cues are a powerful sense for most people, and the earliest stories were spoken aloud rather than written. Use sound to evoke metaphoric feeling—the longing of a train whistle, for example, or the harsh clanging of a locomotive. If you re-create sound effectively on the page, there's no need to name the emotion you're trying to convey, because the auditory cue

will serve as metaphor or, perhaps, actually sound like the feeling you're trying to convey (onomatopoeia).

Smell and taste: The most primitive or limbic of our senses, odors and
tastes, can resurrect the past. Are there foods that take you back to the first
time you tasted them, smells that place you in a moment from your past? Pick
one and write about it.

Objects: As Alfred Hitchcock showed us in movies like *Suspicion* (where
the glowing glass of possibly poisoned milk in Cary Grant's hand signifies
murderous intentions), an object strategically placed can stand in for events
or emotional changes and transport us to another moment. Try thinking of
an object as fodder for a cinematic quick cut in your memoir and see where
it takes you. Even something as simple as a screen door can open (pun
intended) into possibility.

Reading: Choose a memoir and record your impressions of how details of
place affect the action and mood in one or more chapters. How do details of
landscape highlight certain experiences in the memoir? Are there images that
recur and acquire symbolic power? How is that achieved? List aspects of
social and cultural environment that are also revealed.

Writing: Create a visual representation for a sequence in your story: on a large
piece of paper, map where the key events in your story occur. Insert images or
metaphors that bring the place to life. Feel free to draw pictures and circle
words. You may want to visually trace the connections between your various
characters or graph the arc of the plot as well. In this way, you may discover a
key setting where your story comes together or pulls apart. In any case, you'll
discover new correspondences by activating your visual sense with the physicality of drawing and writing.

Reading: From the memoir you chose in the last spotlight exercise on setting,
isolate passages that show action in ways that highlight psychological action
as opposed to physical action. For example, look at how the narrator's reflections move the story along in a particular scene. How does word choice play
a part in addition to rhythm and mood?

Writing: Construct a scene using only dialogue between two characters. How
can you show each character listening as well as talking? How can the dialogue show relationship? Conflict?

Reading and writing: Explore a moment of silence in a memoir of your choosing. How does the author use words, the lack of words, rhythm, or repetition

to convey silence or cessation of time? Now imagine a silent moment in your story and construct three versions, one using gesture only, one using description, and the last using rhythm and/or repetition. Which example most fully telegraphs your intention?

Chapter 6. Your Story, Your Voice

Writing: If you've written at all, you already know your writing voice sounds different from your speaking voice. For this exercise, you'll need a recording device (your computer or phone may well have one). Pick a story from your past you know well, perhaps one that you've told many times but have never written down. Without any preparation (no time for worry—just do it!), record the story, with the understanding that no one but you will ever listen to this recording. You're recording it only for the purpose of this exercise.

Don't play back the recording immediately after you've made it. Instead, move on to the next step in this exercise and write down the story. You may find yourself crossing things out (or, if you're typing, deleting them) as well as moving words or even sentences around. That's fine—this is the written version, and that's precisely what writers do. Take your time, perhaps even going back to polish your draft the next day.

When you've finished this written draft, print out a hard copy. Now comes the point of all this. Have one or more colored pens or pencils ready, then play back the recording. Using different colors for different nuances (red for word choice, for example, or blue for elision or expansion), note where what's on the page differs from what you say in the recording.

Next, consider the differences between these two versions. Are there different word choices—"lovely" instead of "awesome," for example? Did you phrase your sentences more formally or reorder the telling to enhance its effect? Did you, like Williams, shift into another person to make a point? Maybe in the written version you chose to give more detail about a particular moment or realized that another moment didn't need to be there at all. Each of these differences between your spoken voice and your written one is a hallmark of your writing voice. Practicing the hallmarks you discover in this exercise can help you make your writer's voice still stronger and more distinct.

Reading: Analyze a section from one of the books mentioned in this chapter and reflect on how the use of first, second, or third person affects your involvement as a reader.

Writing: One of the advantages of writing about your experiencing self in the third person is that it can help you approach material you've found difficult to write about until now. For this exercise, select an embarrassing moment from your past—preferably something you've never shared with anyone. Next, give the experiencing you a name—make her a character, in other words. Finally, create a scene for that character, using the embarrassing moment as its basis. Allow what really happened *and your emotions* about the scene—both then and now—free rein on the page. After all, you're not writing about *you* anymore but about your *character*.

When you've finished, put the scene away until the next day. When you do read the piece, see if you've gotten closer to the character-you (and his emotions) by using the third person. We'll bet you have. Writing in the third person allows us to approach problematic moments that are even now difficult to acknowledge.

If this is a scene that your memoir needs, you can now rewrite it using the first person. Or you may choose to keep it in third person or even experiment with second. The important thing is to get every scene that's intrinsic to your story on the page. Changing person can help you do so.

Writing: Seeing visceral details through a camera's eye can help you convey their emotional weight. To try this yourself, pick a scene from your childhood where you are observing adults. Make notes to answer the following: Where are you? Where are they? What is going on? How do you feel about the physical presence of the adults in your view? Give a visceral detail for each that conveys your emotional response as well. To extend the exercise, write the scene in first person and then in third person. Compare the effect of each.

Chapter 7. Honoring the Memoir Process

Writing: Who are the voices in your head? Are they encouraging you? If so, what are they saying? Write down their words of encouragement. Or, conversely, are they trying to stop you from telling your story? If that's the case, write down who these voices are and the roadblocks they're putting in your way. By identifying how others feel about your story, you honor *their* place in *your* story. Either way, whether the voices in your head are cheering you on or creating self-doubt, you must assert your right to speak and claim your story.

Glossary

An *autobiography* is a record of a life.

A story's *catalyst* is a specific incident that illuminates the occasion of the telling and sets the story in motion.

Conflict occurs when someone wants something that he or she doesn't get or when a character is blocked.

The *denotative meaning* of a word is its dictionary meaning; the *connotative meaning* includes implied characteristics found in the word's context.

In a sentence or utterance, *diction* refers to the choice of words and style of enunciation.

Dominant images and *sustaining metaphors* gather momentum as the story moves forward, like the proverbial snowball rolling down the hill. Through accretion of key images and metaphors, mood and tone are set by the writer and communicated to the reader. See also *scaffolding*.

Dramatic structure organizes both scenes and the larger work into a coherent whole that moves forward from its opening moment. (1) The *catalyst* is the moment in time at which a scene begins to move. (2) The *conflict* involves the oppositions, internal or external, facing the protagonist. (3) The *rising action* deepens the oppositions the protagonist faces. (4) The *climax* is a scene's epiphanic moment—the turn, the shift, the pivot point. (5) The *denouement* provides closure.

The *emblematic moment* is an image or complex of images metaphorical of a larger truth in the story.

Emblematic scenes not only highlight a particular moment but represent the memoir's larger themes as well, moving the action forward while also serving as microcosms and metaphors for the larger work.

An *epiphany* is a moment of realization or heightened awareness that can lead to change in the protagonist.

The *experiencing self* refers to the author in the past.

Imagery refers to the sensory details of sound, taste, and smell as well as the visual details that provide the reader with an experiential quality.

Implied author refers to the imagined person behind the narrative voice of a work as opposed to the actual author of that work. The implied author is created, just as the work itself is.

A *leitmotif* is a complex metaphor layered into the story; it builds associations around a person, place, or thing.

A *memoir* is an exploration of a significant time in a life using narrative strategies to create a dynamic story.

A *metaphor* connects two unrelated things and creates a relationship between them. The phrase "the chasm of despair," for example, lends an emotional tone and a physical image to an abstract noun.

Milieu refers to the social environment and often the ambience of a setting. It can reference a historical time as well as the values of an era or an author.

The *occasion of the telling* answers the question, Why is *this* story being told now?

Plot is the dramatic sequencing of events in your story.

Point of view refers to the assumed eyes and ears of the "person" telling a story. In the case of memoir, this is almost always you.

A memoir's *preface* often connects the two yous.

A *reliable* narrator appears to have a perspective in line with the values in the story and is someone the reader trusts to have a balanced view of the story.

The *remembering self* refers to the author in the present.

Reversals are unexpected events that send the narrative in a new direction.

Scaffolding refers to the metaphoric connections of disparate events in a story to create a larger, more resonant meaning.

Scenes are moments in motion whose developing action (internal or external) engages and keeps the reader's interest.

Sensory cues employ a scent, taste, or touch to trigger a flashback.

We use the term *speaker* or *narrator* when we discuss the voice that relates to a memoir in order to distance the writer from his or her characters, even or especially when the writer is a character.

Story arc refers to the movement among the elements of dramatic structure that form a narrative. See also *dramatic structure*.

Structure is the framework that contains your story (and includes plot). (1) In an *associative structure*, the scenes are linked by a quality, a mood, a connection. This structure feels "natural," as memory itself arises from such cues or triggers. (2) In a *chronological structure*, events unfold in linear time. (3) In a *circular structure*, a key or catalyzing incident serves as an anchor for the story; the narrator returns to it again and again. (4) A *collage structure* juxtaposes discrete events against one another; the reader fills in the gaps, making meaning by forging connections between events that seem unrelated. (5) A *locational structure* uses place or setting to ground the various segments of the narrative. (6) A ***parallel structure*** contrasts two time periods and often two people, creating deeper meaning via a rich, parallel narrative.

Style refers to the sound of the voice on the page: its tone, rhythm, and way of speaking.

Subtext exists beneath the surface of the story and is shown via detail, dialogue, and scene, revealing (in Charles Baxter's words) its "chronic tensions."

A ***symbol*** refers to a word or concept developed through context and layered by repetition so that it takes on larger meaning.

Syntax refers to the arrangement of the words in a sentence or utterance.

Time is telegraphed in narrative by the following elements: (1) A ***scene*** takes place in actual time. Because it contains largely dialogue with minimal reaction, the pacing of a scene reflects the amount of time that such an interchange might actually take. (2) A ***summary*** is a collapsing of time, as in "four years later . . ." The writer makes a transition to let the reader know where he or she is in time, but the brief mention of time is vastly shorter than the chronicling of "four years" or whatever chunk of time the writer is referencing. (3) A ***description*** expands time. The writer may linger on a moment that in the thinking could be a flash but that in the telling is leisurely. Description arrests time and allows for psychological detail as well.

Tone refers to the overall mood of a story or a scene. It is the emotional coloring a writer creates through language, events, and rhythm.

The ***two yous*** refers to you, the remembering self, now, and you, the experiencing self, then.

An ***unreliable narrator*** deceives himself or the reader—his view of events does not mesh with the "facts" of what really happened. An unreliable narrator forces the reader to decide for herself what the story's truth really is.

Voice refers to the sound of the narrator on the page. More nuanced and sophisticated than your regular speaking voice, your voice on the page is the you who can best tell *this* story.

Bibliography

Abbey, Edward. *Desert Solitaire: A Season in the Wilderness.* New York: Ballantine, 1990.

Atwood, Margaret. *Moral Disorder: Stories.* New York: Nan A. Talese/Doubleday, 2006.

———. *Negotiating with the Dead: A Writer on Writing.* New York: Cambridge University Press, 2002.

Barrington, Judith. *Writing the Memoir: From Truth to Art.* Portland: Eighth Mountain Press, 2002.

Bartók, Mira. *The Memory Palace: A Memoir.* New York: Free Press, 2011.

Baxter, Charles. *The Art of Subtext: Beyond Plot.* Saint Paul, MN: Graywolf Press, 2007.

Beckett, Samuel. *Waiting for Godot: Tragicomedy in 2 Acts.* New York: Grove Press, 1954.

Birkerts, Sven. *The Art of Time in Memoir: Then, Again.* Saint Paul, MN: Graywolf Press, 2009.

Butler, Robert Olen. *From Where You Dream: The Process of Writing Fiction.* New York: Grove Press, 2005.

Carlson, Ron. *Ron Carlson Writes a Story.* Saint Paul, MN: Graywolf Press, 2007.

Cather, Willa. *Death Comes for the Archbishop.* New York: Alfred A Knopf, 1927.

Childs, Craig. *The Desert Cries: A Season of Flash Floods in a Dry Land.* Singapore: Arizona Highways Books, 2002.

deBuys, William. *The Walk.* San Antonio: Trinity University Press, 2007.

Didion, Joan. *The Year of Magical Thinking.* New York: Alfred A. Knopf, 2005.

Dillard, Annie. *An American Childhood.* New York: Perennial Library, 1988.

———. "To Fashion a Text." In *Inventing the Truth: The Art and Craft of Memoir,* edited by William Zinsser, 141–61. Boston: Houghton-Mifflin, 1987.

Doty, Mark. *Heaven's Coast: A Memoir.* New York: HarperCollins, 1996.

Erlich, Gretel. *The Solace of Open Spaces.* New York: Penguin, 1985.

Frazier, Ian. "Looking for My Family." In *Inventing the Truth: The Art and Craft of Memoir*, edited by William Zinsser, 163–81. Boston: Houghton-Mifflin, 1987.

Freed, Lynn. *Reading, Writing, and Leaving Home: Life on the Page*. New York: Harcourt, 2005.

Frey, James. *A Million Little Pieces*. New York: Nan A. Talese/Doubleday, 2003.

Furman, Laura. *Ordinary Paradise*. Houston: Winedale Publishing, 1998.

García Márquez, Gabriel. *Vivir para contarla*. Barcelona: Mondadori, 2002.

Gates, Henry Louis, Jr. "Lifting the Veil." In *Inventing the Truth: The Art and Craft of Memoir*, edited by William Zinsser, 101–18. Boston: Houghton-Mifflin, 1987.

Gerard, Philip. *Creative Nonfiction: Researching and Crafting Stories of Real Life*. Cincinnati: Story Press Books, 1996.

Gilbert, Elizabeth. *Eat, Pray, Love: One Woman's Search for Everything across Italy, India and Indonesia*. New York: Penguin, 2007.

Goldberg, Natalie. *Writing Down the Bones: Freeing the Writer Within*. Boston: Shambhala, 1985.

Gornick, Vivian. *The Situation and the Story: The Art of Personal Narrative*. New York: Farrar, Straus and Giroux, 2001.

Gutkind, Lee. *The Art of Creative Nonfiction: Writing and Selling the Literature of Reality*. New York: John Wiley & Sons, 1997.

Hadas, Rachel. *Strange Relation: A Memoir of Marriage, Dementia, and Poetry*. Philadelphia: Paul Dry Books, 2011.

Hall, Donald. "Bring Back the Out-Loud Culture." *Newsweek*, April 15, 1985, 12.

Hampl, Patricia. *I Could Tell You Stories: Sojourns in the Land of Memory*. New York: W. W. Norton, 1995.

———. *A Romantic Education*. New York: W. W. Norton, 1981.

Hampl, Patricia, and Elaine Tyler May, eds. *Tell Me True: Memoir, History, and Writing a Life*. Saint Paul, MN: Borealis Books, 2008.

Hijuelos, Oscar. *Thoughts without Cigarettes: A Memoir*. New York: Gotham Books, 2011.

Kaplan, Alice. "Lady of the Lake." In *Tell Me True: Memoir, History, and Writing a Life*, edited by Patricia Hampl and Elaine Tyler May, 97–114. St. Paul, MN: Borealis Books, 2008.

Karr, Mary. *The Liars' Club: A Memoir*. New York: Viking, 1995.

Lamb, Nancy. *The Art and Craft of Storytelling: A Comprehensive Guide to Classic Writing Techniques*. Cincinnati: Writer's Digest Books, 2008.

Lenard-Cook, Lisa. *The Mind of Your Story: Discover What Drives Your Fiction*. Cincinnati: Writer's Digest Books, 2008.

Link, Aaron Raz, and Hilda Raz. *What Becomes You*. Lincoln: University of Nebraska Press, 2007.

Lively, Penelope. *Making It Up*. New York: Viking, 2005.

———. *Oleander, Jacaranda: A Childhood Perceived*. New York: HarperCollins, 1994.

Lord, Albert B. *The Singer of Tales*. New York: Atheneum, 1976.

Mars, Julie. *A Month of Sundays: Searching for the Spirit and My Sister*. Pine Bush, NY: GreyCore, 2005.

McCourt, Frank. *Angela's Ashes: A Memoir*. New York: Simon & Shuster, 1996.

Meloy, Ellen. *Eating Stone: Imagination and the Loss of the Wild*. New York: Vintage, 2005.

Morrison, Toni. "The Site of Memory." In *Inventing the Truth: The Art and Craft of Memoir*, edited by William Zinsser, 185–200. Boston: Houghton-Mifflin, 1987.

Mortensen, Greg. *Three Cups of Tea: One Man's Mission to Promote Peace—One School at a Time*. New York: Penguin Books, 2007.

Miller, Lynn C., Jacqueline Taylor, and M. Heather Carver, eds. *Voices Made Flesh: Performing Women's Autobiography*. Madison: University of Wisconsin Press, 2003.

Norton, Lisa Dale. *Shimmering Images: A Handy Little Guide to Writing Memoir*. New York: St. Martin's, 2009.

Nguyen, Bich Minh. *Stealing Buddha's Dinner: A Memoir*. New York: Penguin, 2007.

Oates, Joyce Carol. *A Widow's Tale: A Memoir*. New York: Ecco, 2011.

Oliver, Mary. *Long Life: Essays and Other Writings*. Cambridge: Da Capo, 2004.

O'Rourke, Meghan. *The Long Goodbye*. New York: Riverhead, 2011.

Pinter, Harold. *Betrayal*. New York: Grove, 1994.

Powell, Julie. *Julie and Julia: 365 Days, 524 Recipes, 1 Tiny Apartment Kitchen*. New York: Little, Brown, 2005.

Prose, Francine. *Reading Like a Writer: A Guide for People Who Love Books and for Those Who Want to Write Them*. New York: HarperCollins, 2006.

Russell, Sharman Apt. *Standing in the Light: My Life as a Pantheist*. New York: Basic Books, 2008.

Sargent, Marcia J. *Wing Wife: How to Be Married to a Fighter Pilot*. Laguna Beach: CreateSpace, 2010.

Sexton, Linda Gray. *Searching for Mercy Street: My Journey Back to My Mother, Anne Sexton*. Boston: Little, Brown, 1994.

Shapiro, Dani. *Slow Motion: A Memoir of a Life Rescued by Tragedy*. New York: Harper Perennial, 2010.

Silverman, Sue William. *Fearless Confessions: A Writer's Guide to Memoir*. Athens: University of Georgia Press, 2009.

Smith, Patti. *Just Kids*. New York: HarperCollins, 2010.

Smith, Sidonie. *A Poetics of Women's Autobiography: Marginality and the Fictions of Self-Representation*. Bloomington: Indiana University Press, 1987.

Stegner, Wallace. *On the Teaching of Creative Writing: Responses to a Series of Questions*. Hanover: University Press of New England, 1988.

Stein, Gertrude. *Lectures in America*. New York: Random House, 1935.

Thomas, Abigail. *Safekeeping: Some True Stories from a Life*. New York: Anchor, 2000.

———. *A Three Dog Life*. Orlando: Harcourt, 2006.

Vargas Llosa, Mario. *A Writer's Reality.* Syracuse, NY: Syracuse University Press, 1991.

Walls, Jeannette. *The Glass Castle.* 2005. Reprint, New York: Scribner, 2006.

Weimer, Joan. *Back Talk: Teaching Lost Selves to Speak.* Chicago: University of Chicago Press, 1994.

Welty, Eudora. *One Writer's Beginnings.* New York: Warner Books, 1983.

Williams, Terry Tempest. *Refuge: An Unnatural History of Family and Place.* New York: Vintage, 1992.

Wolff, Geoffrey. *The Duke of Deception: Memories of My Father.* New York: Vintage, 1979.

Wolff, Tobias. *This Boy's Life: A Memoir.* New York: Grove/Atlantic, 1989.

Zailckas, Koren. *Fury: A Memoir.* New York: Viking, 2010.

Zinsser, William, ed. *Inventing the Truth: The Art and Craft of Memoir.* Boston: Houghton Mifflin, 1987.

Other Suggested Memoirs

Beah, Ishmael. *A Long Way Gone: Memoirs of a Boy Soldier*. New York: Farrar, Straus and Giroux, 2008.

Caldwell, Gail. *Let's Take the Long Way Home: A Memoir of Friendship*. New York: Random House, 2010.

Capote, Truman. *Other Voices, Other Rooms*. New York: Signet, 1948.

Childs, Craig. *The Secret Knowledge of Water: Discovering the Essence of the American Desert*. New York: Back Bay Books, 2001.

Didion, Joan. *Blue Nights*. New York: Alfred A. Knopf, 2011.

Dillard, Annie. *Pilgrim at Tinker Creek*. New York: Perennial, 1988.

———. *Teaching a Stone to Talk: Expeditions and Encounters*. New York: Harper Perennial, 1992.

———. *Tickets for a Prayer Wheel: Poems*. New York: Harper & Row, 1988.

———. *The Writing Life*. New York: Harper, 1990.

Doig, Ivan. *This House of Sky: Landscapes of a Western Mind*. New York: Harcourt Brace Jovanovich, 1980.

Doty, Mark. *Dog Years: A Memoir*. New York: HarperCollins, 2007.

Fox, Paula. *Borrowed Finery: A Memoir*. New York: Picador, 2001.

Fuller, Alexandra. *Don't Let's Go to the Dogs Tonight: An African Childhood*. New York: Random House, 2011.

Grogan, John. *Marley and Me: Life and Love with the World's Worst Dog*. New York: Harper Perennial, 2008.

Howard, Blanche, and Allison Howard, eds. *A Memoir of Friendship: The Letters between Carol Shields and Blanche Howard*. Toronto: Viking Canada, 2007.

Karr, Mary. *Lit: A Memoir*. New York: HarperCollins, 2009.

Kennedy, Edward. *True Compass: A Memoir*. New York: Twelve, 2009.

Kingston, Maxine Hong. *The Woman Warrior: Memoirs of a Girlhood among Ghosts*. New York: Vintage, 1977.

Klein, Gerda Weissman. *All but My Life*. New York: Hill & Wang, 1957.

Knapp, Caroline. *Drinking: A Love Story*. New York: Bantam Doubleday Dell, 1996.

Koller, Alice. *An Unknown Woman*. New York: Bantam, 1991.

Lagnado, Lucette. *The Man in the White Sharkskin Suit: A Jewish Family's Exodus from Old Cairo to the New World*. New York: Harper Perennial, 2008.

Laurence, Margaret. *The Prophet's Camel Bell*. Toronto: McClelland & Stewart, 1963.

Levi, Primo. *The Periodic Table*. New York: Everyman's Library, 1996.

Moore, Lucy. *Into the Canyon: Seven Years in Navajo Country*. Albuquerque: University of New Mexico Press, 2004.

Morris, Mary. *Nothing to Declare: Memoirs of a Woman Traveling Alone*. New York: Picador, 1988.

Nabokov, Vladimir. *Speak Memory: An Autobiography Revisited*. New York: Alfred A. Knopf, 1999.

Obama, Barack. *Dreams from My Father: A Story of Race and Inheritance*. New York: Crown, 2007.

Pamuk, Orhan. *Istanbul: Memories and the City*. New York: Alfred A. Knopf, 2006.

Perillo, Lucia. *I've Heard the Vultures Singing: Field Notes on Poetry, Illness, and Nature*. Dallas: Trinity University Press, 2009.

Rodriguez, Richard. *Hunger of Memory: The Education of Richard Rodriguez*. New York: Bantam, 1983.

Rudner, Ruth. *Ask Now the Beasts: Our Kinship with Animals Wild and Domestic*. New York: Marlowe, 2006.

Saks, Elyn R. *The Center Cannot Hold: My Journey through Madness*. New York: Hyperion, 2007.

Scheeres, Julia. *Jesus Land: A Memoir*. New York: Counterpoint, 2006.

Sedaris, David. *Me Talk Pretty One Day*. New York: Little, Brown, 2000.

Silko, Leslie Marmon. *Storyteller*. New York: Little, Brown, 1981.

Skloot, Floyd. *In the Shadow of Memory*. Lincoln, NE: Bison Books, 2004.

Smith, Annick. *Homestead*. Minneapolis: Milkweed, 1995.

Spark, Debra. *Curious Attractions: Essays on Fiction Writing*. Ann Arbor: University of Michigan Press, 2005.

Steinbeck, John. *Travels with Charley: In Search of America*. New York: Penguin, 1962.

Styron, William. *Darkness Visible: A Memoir of Madness*. New York: Vintage, 1990.

Taylor, Jacqueline. *Waiting for the Call: From Preacher's Daughter to Lesbian Mom*. Ann Arbor: University of Michigan Press, 2007.

Taylor, Jill Bolte. *My Stroke of Insight: A Brain Scientist's Personal Journey*. New York: Plume, 2009.

Wiesel, Elie. *Night*. Rev. ed. New York: Hill & Wang, 2006.